AWAKENING SPIRIT, FREEING THE WILL

Working with Rudolf Steiner's
Intuitive Thinking as a Spiritual Path
The Philosophy of Freedom

Hugh Renwick, M.A.
Wilton, NH

PUBLICATIONS

Awakening Spirit, Freeing the Will
Working with Rudolf Steiner's
Intuitive Thinking as a Spiritual Path
The Philosophy of Freedom

Cover Painting: "American Earth," 2014, oil, earth, pigments, and marble dust, by Martina Angela Müller.

Waldorf Publications
ISBN 978-1-943582-64-8

at the Research Institute for Waldorf Education (RIWE)
351 Fairview Avenue, Unit 625
Hudson, NY 12534
www.waldorfresearchinstitute.org
For purchase at www.WaldorfPublications.org

 PUBLICATIONS

Table of Contents

Foreword...5

Preface 7

Introduction..9

The Knowledge of Freedom 17

The Reality of Freedom 47

Final Questions..95

Conclusion 101

Foreword

The Self-Sustaining Power of Creative Thinking:
An Essay on Rudolf Steiner's Philosophy of Freedom

In his study guide to Rudolf Steiner's *Philosophy of Freedom*, Hugh Renwick actually practices what Steiner wanted readers to do: namely, to work the book through and meditate on it in such a way that they render its insights anew. Hugh has done this by updating Steiner's seminal text with contemporary examples and fresh insights concerning the vital question of whether or not human beings are really free. Above all, in going through Hugh's essay one encounters not only new philosophical insights, but, even more importantly, one discovers in one's own thinking new mental/spiritual capacities.

Awakening Spirit, Freeing the Will is of particular value for the personal and professional development of teachers. In his essay, Hugh develops illustrative examples that facilitate access to Steiner's sometimes complex philosophical and cognitive ideas. As a former Waldorf high school and elementary teacher, he is able to describe, for example, how one can apply Steiner's central theme of "moral intuition" in the classroom. One of his own experiences of the freedom attained through "moral intuition" is vividly described in a classroom incident in which he freed his thinking of preconceived notions in order to meet the needs of a particularly restless child. Another guiding image captures Steiner's "One-World-Philosophy" (his Monism) by analogy to recent research on the interconnectedness of trees and other forest organisms.

As a former class teacher myself, who over the years has periodically revisited Steiner's work individually and in faculty study, I have come to appreciate how *The Philosophy of Freedom* actually embodies the central idea of the "education towards freedom" Steiner initiated in 1919. During 2020, the year of "Zooming", I had the opportunity to read through and discuss Hugh's new rendering with him as a research partner. In the course of our conversations, it became clear to me how Steiner encapsulated the essence of his *Philosophy of Freedom* (1894) in the first of two Teacher Meditations he gave many years later to help teachers prepare their lessons. This meditation poetically describes how the surrounding sensory world embodies a wisdom and hidden power into which we as teachers can tap if we so will. The key is to link this power with our own inner life, in our "I," where a like source of strength resides in our thinking and capacity of imagination. When enhanced, thinking can unite us with this "world-wisdom" and thereby release in us the insight and strength needed to do our work. Steiner's central epistemological concepts of percept and concept become in this meditation "the shining of the senses" and "thinking's revelation."

Midway through this meditation, a pivotal reference is made to our thinking *as supporting itself with its own strength* ("auf eigener Kraft sich stutzend"), a central theme in Steiner's philosophy. By drawing attention to thinking's own power, Steiner is pointing to the necessary step we must take to experience our thinking as an independent and unconditioned source of mental/spiritual energy and freed will. This does not mean that a thinker becomes isolated in a solipsistic world, but rather that he or she freely chooses to unite this activity with the world for the good of all. In other words, we come, as teachers, to know and trust our thinking as an objective and creative instrument that can serve our students and those around us. Hugh Renwick's *Awakening Spirit, Freeing the Will* is a welcome aid to help teachers and other professionals in this endeavor.

Arthur Auer
Christmas, 2020

Preface

In 1894 the Austrian philosopher, Rudolf Steiner, published a book that he entitled *The Philosophy of Freedom*, recently translated from the German as *Intuitive Thinking as a Spiritual Path, A Philosophy of Freedom*. The main purpose of this book was to explain how one can achieve what has traditionally been referred to as a "free will." For centuries, philosophers have argued for and against the existence of free will, or, in other words, the possibility of achieving true freedom in our actions. Not long after Rudolf Steiner earned a doctorate in philosophy, he added his thoughts to this age-old debate, and his book has been through many editions since then, right up to the present.

During his lifetime, Steiner wrote many books on philosophical and spiritual topics. He gave hundreds of lectures throughout Europe, initiated new research and development in various fields including medicine, agriculture, economics, and education, and founded the first Waldorf School, implementing his method for elementary and secondary education. He often referred to his *Philosophy of Freedom* and recommended its study as a means of intellectual and moral development. With that recommendation in mind, I wrote this essay to make clear to myself Steiner's argument in his book, against the backdrop of the contemporary debate concerning free will. I offer it as a resource for anyone interested in studying Steiner's text and his philosophical orientation in general.

In this essay I attempt to summarize Steiner's text in my own words. I have not included all the content of the book in this summary, only what I have thought to be the most essential content in following his reasoning. I cite relevant quotations where I believe them to be helpful, and I add my own commentary and examples in certain places that have helped me to interpret and understand his meaning.

HR

Introduction

Who in our modern world does not want to be free? From childhood and adolescence onwards, the desire to be free from external constraints and controls is felt by everyone at least to some degree. And as we mature, the desire to be free *to do as we choose* grows stronger and stronger in us. We feel entitled to choose our friends, life partners, occupation, place of residence, style of home, not to mention our dress and manner of appearance. Nevertheless, we also feel the need to conform to our surroundings, current fads, and cultural norms. As the Danish philosopher Soren Kierkegaard once pointed out, for many people it is not how much freedom you can *get*, it is how much you can stand. And along with freedom comes responsibility to act appropriately and without doing harm to self and others. To be completely and responsibly free, in fact, does not come easily, and many people question if it is even possible.

The age-old debate as to whether or not the human will is free continues to this day. In his book mentioned in the Preface above, Rudolf Steiner (1861-1925) added an important line of thought to this debate. For him the real issue is not whether we are naturally endowed with free will but how we can *achieve* it, given that in so many respects our will is conditioned and determined according to our biological necessities, cultural environment, personal habits, and psychological conditioning.

The will is central to human being. The word refers to our power to act *intentionally*. Free will refers to actions carried out by ourselves according to our *own* aims and intentions. When we will, we set ourselves in motion. We aim into the future to achieve our aims. And, if our will is strong, we stay the course until our goals are achieved. But how can we be sure that our intentions and actions are truly free?

Upon reflection, we can see that at least part of our intentional activity is unfree. We have physical needs we *must* meet to survive, to make life sustainable. Such needs require us to act. We have no choice in the matter, short of ending our life. Acknowledging and modifying this basic necessity, we may try to embellish those needs with comforts or aesthetic qualities that please us or, on the other hand, to simplify our lives by limiting our needs to the basics—just enough food, adequate simple shelter, a few clothes, and enough money. We still have to satisfy our physical needs, but we can at least decide how to do it, expressing a degree of freedom of choice. In regard to the rest of life, we may well wonder whether our cultural background and psychological conditioning rule over us in as compelling a way as does our biology. Is there any area in which we can be sure that we are acting freely, with no external or internal compulsion?

Those philosophers and psychologists who call themselves determinists argue that the human will is never free. For example, B.F. Skinner (*Beyond Freedom and Dignity*, 1971) applied his stimulus-response model to all of human behavior. In his view, human action is always a response to some stimulus from the environment that causes it. Human character and activity are entirely shaped by environmental factors. Other contemporary philosophers have asserted the same point of view, claiming that our biological needs, our social and cultural environment, our genetic endowment, and our brain functions are all compelling factors of our activity.

Professor Sam Harris (*Free Will*, 2012), is a contemporary philosopher who argues that there are only two ways in which to regard our willed actions. They are 1) either determined by a long chain of causes stretching back in time, which affect our genetic make-up, our brain functions and our upbringing, or 2) they are completely random, with no rational explanation possible. In both cases we are not acting intentionally and freely.

I quote him here briefly:

> Free will *is* an illusion. Our wills are simply not of our own making. Thoughts and intentions emerge from background causes of which we are unaware and over which we exert no conscious control. We do not have the freedom we think we have....... Seeming acts of volition merely arise spontaneously (whether caused, uncaused, or probabilistically inclined, it makes no difference) and cannot be traced to a point of origin in our conscious minds.[1]

Thus Harris does not believe it possible for us to freely *originate* an aim and an action. Every aim, every action we perform, even the random ones, ultimately come from somewhere other than our conscious intention.

A significant result of this way of thinking is that humans cannot be held responsible for their actions. To a limited extent, this assumption is actually built into our legal system in cases concerned with "crimes of passion" or crimes resulting from psychological disorders. Such crimes are often given lighter sentences, specific therapies, or are excused. But our legal system also assumes that most criminal, or otherwise unlawful, actions have been freely intended, which implies that the offenders are responsible for their actions. For the most part, our legal system and that of many other nations are not based on philosophical determinism. Modern democracies are, after all, based on the ideal of freedom for all and the belief that most people are capable of acting freely. We assume that all people have the right to choose how they want to live and can do so responsibly. Laws are in place to ensure we can exercise that right. The rights listed in the constitutions of the world's democratic countries

---

1   Harris, Free Will, p. 5-6

all assume that most people are capable of free and responsible willing.

Our democratic ethos is supported by some contemporary philosophers who, like Professor D.C. Dennett (*Freedom Evolves*, 2003), argue that the human will is capable of free activity and who define this freedom as the ability *to choose* our aims, to freely act on them and to control ourselves from doing harm. In his view, this ability has gradually developed in conjunction with the evolving human brain that serves us.

Dennett is known as a "compatibilist" in regard to the current free will debate. He believes that his view is actually compatible with determinism. For example, he agrees with the determinists that the brain initiates actions from its motor centers and that self-control depends on the development of the prefrontal lobes of the brain. While determinists conclude from this that we are not free to act as we want, since the brain is in control, Dennett counters that we are nonetheless free simply because the brain is part of us. The "I" in the statement "I act freely from my own intentions" refers to all of a person, including our brains, *of which we make use*. To Harris this makes no sense, given his conviction that the controlling brain is itself determined in its actions by our genome, cultural and environmental conditioning, and ingrained habits. As he puts it, "compatibilism amounts to nothing more than the following creed: A puppet is free as long as he loves his strings."[2]

There is a third point of view represented in the current academic debate, that of the "libertarians."[3] Professor Robert Kane (*Free Will*, 2003), a proponent of this view, prefers to call himself a "causal indeterminist," meaning that our willed actions are not predetermined as long as they result from conscious deliberation among a number of possibilities before acting. Furthermore, a person capable of free will has achieved a certain level of self-development, a level on which he has been able *to form his own character*. Hence his character is not predetermined by his genome, upbringing, and other

2 Harris, ibid., p. 20

3 This term, used by academic philosophers, is not related to its use in politics as far as I know.

conditions: he is a free agent able to choose his motives and to be his own source of motivation. As he puts it, such a person is capable of "ultimate control—he originative control exercised by agents when it is "up to them," which of a set of possible choices or actions will now occur, and up to no one and nothing else over which the agents do not also have control."[4]

Professor Alfred Mele (*Free*, 2014), another contemporary libertarian, also points to our human capacity to make conscious choices on our own as the condition for achieving an act of free will. It is clear to him that we can do so, as long we are not subject to excessive force.[5] Both Mele and Kane base their argument for free will on our ability, *once developed*, to make our own conscious choices.

Opposed to this point of view are some contemporary natural scientists, such as biologist Read Montague, who thinks that libertarian views are based on the unfounded assumption of the existence in us of a non-physical "soul" or "spirit."[6] That is, the possibility of free will depends on this assumption of a soul or spirit in us capable of transforming and developing personal character and rising above and controlling all physical and emotional factors affecting our action, including the brain and nervous system. For them, such an assumption is "magical thinking," for it is not verifiable by empirical scientific investigation, limited as it is to the material world. They share the view, similar to that of Sam Harris, that the source of our intentional acts can only be found scientifically in what can be observed of our *physical* being, namely the brain and the neural processes, which are involved in all our sensing, thinking, and motor activity. Given this view, it is not surprising that contemporary science has come to think of the brain as being programmed like a computer, whose "program" consists of chains of ingrained or learned responses and directions, like computer code, rather than being controlled by an assumed soul or spirit who is "in charge" within us.

4   Kane, "Free Will" in Free Will, (Blackwell, 2003) p. 243
5   Mele, Free, Oxford University Press, (New York, 2014), 77f.
6   Montague, *Current Biology*, 2008, p. 584. Mele, op. cit. p.84

These scientists and philosophers make clear the central question in the free will debate today: the question of our human identity. Are we soul and spirit beings as well as physical beings? Does the physical brain rule us like a computer or are we beings who make use of the brain and its processes? Is there a spiritual element in us that is non-material and can be perceived and verified as the source of our thinking and willing?

Rudolf Steiner meant to answer this fundamental question in his *Philosophy of Freedom*. There he indicates how a person can perceive and affirm his spiritual being and, from that center, bring about the personal development needed to achieve free acts of will, initiated from his essential, spiritual core. Had he known Robert Kane, I think Steiner would have absolutely agreed with him that we are capable of "ultimate, originative control" of our actions. In this essay, I will describe what I understand to be Steiner's conditions for doing so, thereby enabling us to free our will and live as truly free beings.

Philosophers and psychologists who have studied the human will have traditionally pointed to its two essential elements: aim and motivation. That is, any act of will involves not just the choice of an aim of action but also the motivation to achieve it. In his analysis of volition, Steiner points to different forms, or levels, of motivation and to the different ways in which we form aims for our actions in life, indicating which of these enable a person to free his or her will. For each person, it is then a matter of achieving that level of motivation and of purpose through personal development.

While Steiner undertakes this analysis of willing in his *Philosophy of Freedom*, it is not until the second part of the book that he does this, the part he entitled *The Reality of Freedom*. In the first part of the book, entitled *The Knowledge of Freedom*, he addresses the fundamental question whether it is possible to achieve true, objective knowledge of the world and its contents, including our human nature and capacities. Steiner describes how and why it *is* possible to achieve this knowledge by analyzing and understanding the role of the elements involved in the activity of cognition. In the process, Steiner leads us to experience our spiritual core, the source of this achievement. Thus, Part 1 of Steiner's book is intended in large part to justify epistemologically the conclusions he reaches in Part 2 concerning the realization of free will. Part 1 consists of 7 Chapters; Part 2 consists of 7 Chapters, plus a concluding summary. In the next section of this essay I will summarize what I see to be the main points of Steiner's analysis of our cognitive activity in Part 1 of his book.

The Knowledge of Freedom

1. Conscious Human Action

Steiner begins his study of human volition in Chapter 1 by observing that the possibility of free will depends on the *conscious* direction of our will, it being obvious that unconscious actions are not freely determined. Conscious direction implies our knowing the reasons for our actions, and knowing this depends on our *ability to think*. In other words, any conscious action of our will requires that we think out our reasons, purposes and aims of action. Steiner then proposes to investigate the *nature and origin of our thinking* to shed light on the question of free will. He is aiming to uncover for us the spiritual core of our being, the agent of our thinking, as well as the role thinking plays in achieving our knowledge of self and world.

2. The Fundamental Urge for Knowledge

In his second Chapter, Steiner begins by characterizing the existential situation in which we find ourselves which produces in us the "fundamental urge" to know and understand the world we perceive around us. He refers this urge to our dissatisfaction with the way in which we first perceive the world. Our initial perceptions of the world and our own nature do not lead to an understanding of them. We cannot at first see how our various sense perceptions are related to each other. We wonder if the world itself is a comprehensible world of interrelationships, yet our sense organs *of themselves* do not enable us to grasp it. Therefore we feel ourselves to be disconnected, even "torn away," from the reality that confronts our senses and which *seems to lie outside* our own being and to be independent of us. As Steiner puts it: "We become aware of standing in opposition to the world, as independent beings. The universe appears to us as two opposites: I and world."[7]

Nevertheless, he adds, we also feel that we belong to the world and "this feeling engenders an effort to bridge the opposition." He states that our "spiritual life consists of a continual searching for the unity between the I and the world." He then notes that in the history of philosophy this searching has given rise to two opposing viewpoints, termed Monism and Dualism, both of which have characterized this opposition between "I and world" in terms of an opposition between spirit and matter, two entirely different "realities": the human "I" (or thinker) being spiritual in nature and the rest of the world of experience being material in nature, as experienced through our sensory organs. Because of this supposedly fundamental difference, Dualists have maintained that we cannot bridge the gap, that all attempts to know and understand the nature of the material world are hypothetical and therefore inconclusive. For Monists, on the other hand, it has historically been a question of denying the apparent reality of one of the two poles, be it spirit or matter. This has given rise either to materialistic philosophies that admit the reality only of matter, and interpret our so-called spiritual activity in thinking as a material function of the material brain, an example of which was the philosophy of Steiner's contemporary F. A. Lange. (Determinists like Sam Harris also figure among such philosophers.) Or, it has given rise to Spiritualism, a brand of philosophy that maintains the illusory nature of matter and its processes, an extreme example of which, according to Steiner, is the philosophy of J. G. Fichte.

---

7   Steiner, The Philosophy of Freedom, p. 19

Steiner next notes a fact that the points of view of Dualism and Monism have neglected to consider:

> In regard to all these points of view, we must empha-
> size that the fundamental and primal opposition
> confronts us first *in our own consciousness*. It is we
> who separate ourselves from the native ground of
> nature and place ourselves as "I" in opposition to
> the "world."[8] (my italics)

I understand Steiner to be saying that the supposed opposition of self and world is experienced and conceived *within* consciousness but is then misunderstood as an opposition *between* consciousness and a so-called external world. As we shall see in later Chapters of his book, Steiner finds the solution to the apparent opposition of self and world, (or of spirit and matter, or of subject and object), in the fact that both sides of the opposition are elements that arise *within* the cognitive process of human consciousness, a process that includes and resolves the opposition within itself. In actual fact, the supposed opposites are only *apparently* outside of and over against each other as separate realities.

Nevertheless, Steiner acknowledges that we all experience a feeling of disconnection from the world. He refers to the poet Goethe who imagined Nature to embrace us within herself, despite our feeling of being separate from her. The all embracing unity of Nature, as Goethe poetically conceived her, will be explained by Steiner to be the all embracing ground of our experience of the world: Human Thinking Consciousness. This is hinted at in the following quotation near the end of the Chapter in which he expresses the issue in a somewhat mysterious manner:

"To be sure, we have torn ourselves away from nature, but we must still have taken something with us into our own being. We must seek out this natural being within ourselves, then we shall also rediscover the connection to her.....What is akin to her within us will

---

8   Ibid. p. 25

be our guide..... We wish to descend into the depths of our own being to find there those elements that we have saved in our flight out of nature....... We must come to the point where we can say to ourselves, "Here I am no longer merely "I" . There is something here that is more than "I". [9]

I think Steiner is hinting that if we explore "the depths of our own being," we will discover that we are not in fact separate from nature. We will find that the world (here referred to as nature), supposedly separate and independent of our consciousness, is not in fact separate from consciousness but actually comes to be *within* consciousness in the form of our perceptions and our concepts and ideas. The world we come to know is a product of the cognitive process that takes place within human consciousness. Thus we will discover in our consciousness "something that is more than "I.""

In the Chapters that follow, Steiner will develop his own form of Monism, which, rather than denying the reality of one of the two terms of self and world, or spirit and matter, actually embraces both terms in the process of cognition through which the world as we know it *comes to be* for us.

3. *Thinking in the Service of Understanding the World*

In Chapter 3, Steiner passes on to describe the nature of our thinking as he proposed to do at the end of Chapter 1. He makes several points.

1. Thinking is necessary for us to determine the identity of perceived objects and events, and to understand how they are connected. Simply observing or perceiving the world does not of itself yield knowledge of its various contents, relationships, and laws. To gain knowledge, both observation (perception) and thinking have to be our points of departure.

2. In our everyday cognitive activity, we do not observe our thinking itself. We engage ourselves in the process of thinking about the

---

9 ibid., pp. 25-26

objects and events before us. Ordinarily, our focus is on the objective world and not on our thinking.

3. Normally, we observe our thinking itself only after it has occurred, by reflecting back on it. In doing so, we can realize that when we think, the meanings of our thoughts are "transparent and clear" to us. Reflecting on our thinking, we know *that we have done it* and we know *what* we were thinking. The content of thinking is not hidden from us, and that content can be deepened and corrected overtime. Example: "I used to think that sugar was good for us, but now I know otherwise."

4. The "transparency and clarity" of thinking and thought is not true of sense perceptions. Their meaning (their identity and interrelationships) are not evident until thinking takes hold of them. As soon as we name what we are perceiving, thinking has identified it. Example: "What am I smelling? Ah, burning rubber!"

Steiner gives an example to clarify this last point. His explanation is very brief, and I will expand on it here. When we perceive two events and call them lightning and thunder, we have applied those concepts to our sense perceptions. As concepts we can grasp their meaning and know how they are connected, but we would not know this having simply *perceived* through our eyes and ears their occurrence one after the other, as pure perceptions, without thinking. When we perceive them, our thinking might take the following course: "That was a flash of lightning, as we call it, a powerful example of an electrical discharge, which always involves not just a flash but also a disturbance in the air, resulting in a sounding of some kind. In this case, thunder must be the sounding connected to that very intense discharge, and it reaches us afterwards because of the known fact that sound travels more slowly than light."

These last two sentences represent a conceptualization of the events. While engaged in that thought production, in that thinking process, we do not ordinarily focus on it itself. We are focused outward on the events in question. When we do reflect on our thinking, however, we can see that the meanings of our thoughts or concepts are clear to us. We already know (have learned) what the concepts lightning, electrical discharge, air pressure, and thunder mean and refer to. Those meanings simply and clearly indicate the nature and relationship of the two phenomena observed by means of our sense organs.

Of course, our knowing about such events is not based only on our direct, present-time observation, for we often are not the first to observe and think about them. The concepts involved may well have been discovered by others, and we may well have learned them in school. I think Steiner's point in mentioning them is simply to show that concepts are always involved in our cognitive process and enable us to see and understand the identity and relationships of our sense perceptions.

At this point, Steiner brings up what might be an objection to these reflections concerning our thinking process. Some brain physiologists of his time (and of ours) maintained that it is the physical brain itself that thinks in us, and not an assumed thinking power that makes use of the brain. Rather, they interpret physiological events in the brain as causative of our thoughts and thinking process. To this view, Steiner responds as follows:

> What I observe about thinking is not the process in my brain linking the concepts of lightning and thunder, but rather the process enabling me to bring the two concepts into a specific relationship. Observation tells me that nothing guides me in combining my thoughts except the content of my thoughts. I am not guided by the material processes in my brain.[10]

Steiner is not denying that nerve processes occur in the brain when we think. We can observe them accompanying our thinking. But we do not observe them *doing* the thinking. It is not the brain that comprehends and connects our thoughts: our thinking does, and that we *can* observe.

---

10   Steiner, ibid., p 35

5. Steiner's next point concerns this fact about our thinking activity. Not only can we *not* observe the brain producing our thoughts, we *can* observe ourselves actively involved in thinking. We can observe our *effort* to search for concepts to explain our sense experience as well as our actual process of understanding and expressing in words the relation among the concepts we have formed. This observation of our effort and comprehension may occur after the fact of thinking, as a reflection or even a perception of fatigue or strain. But it can also be observed *in* the act of thinking itself, if we turn our attention to our willed effort and our comprehending *while we are engaged in them.*

At this point in the Chapter, Steiner refers to Eduard von Hartmann, a philosopher of his own time, who maintained that our thinking is only a phenomenal appearance produced by an unconscious activity in the brain. In his view, we cannot therefore observe the real thinking itself, and we are simply fooled into thinking that we are its source. Steiner responds to this view as follows:

> This objection.....fails to take into account that it is the "I" itself that—within thinking—observes *its own* activity. If it could be fooled,........ the "I" would have to be *outside* thinking.[11]

Steiner clearly asks his readers to recognize this fact through self-observation. Once it is clear to me that when thinking occurs, I am doing the thinking, then how could I possibly conclude that my brain is doing the thinking? That would be a self-contradictory thought: I think that I am not doing the thinking that I am doing but am somehow outside of it. How would I know this except through thinking?

6. Based on these last points about thinking (that we can clearly grasp our thoughts and their relationships, and that we ourselves produce our thinking), Steiner now makes his last point in this Chapter. He concludes that thinking provides us with a "firm starting point" for the endeavor to understand the world. But, as he goes

---

11 Steiner, ibid., p 47

on to say, the question now is whether the application of thinking to the world is right or wrong, correct or false. Example: Are we correct in thinking that global warming is causing the melting of the glaciers, or are we mistaken?

The points that Steiner makes in the second and third Chapters have helped me to understand, among other things, just what he means when he uses the pronoun "I". He uses this pronoun to refer to our identity as thinkers. For him, the word "I" is properly used in reference to something more than, even other than, our bodily and feeling nature, although we often identify ourselves with the latter two. Example: I am too fat, or I am happy.

We can experience this "I" in our *activity* of thinking. For Steiner, we *are* the willed effort, that power, that is active in thinking and that comprehends meaning. It is our spiritual, or non-material nature. On this point, Steiner agrees with the philosopher Hegel who stated that "thinking turns the soul, with which animals too are gifted, into spirit." For Steiner, Hegel, and many other philosophers of the Idealist tradition, the term "spirit" refers to both our self-sustaining power to think and the conceptual meanings that we discover and come to understand through thinking. My thinking spirit is the core of my individual identity and it is universal in its scope, for it can, through thinking, come to know all that is given to it.[12]

Steiner states here and later in the text that we can verify for ourselves that we are spiritual, as well as emotional and physical beings, by observing ourselves in our self-produced activity of thinking and knowing. Many people today, as in the past, will object to this view, convinced that it is the brain that thinks in us. Steiner challenges us to observe ourselves as we think, so as to achieve the understanding that he is presenting here.

---

12 Steiner, ibid., p.16

4. The World as Percept

In Chapter 4, Rudolf Steiner continues his investigation into the nature of cognition, the two components of which he has previously indicated to be our observed perceptions and our concepts, arrived at through thinking. He observes that these two components of cognition, or our knowing activity, arise in us as on a "stage"—that is, the stage of our human consciousness. He is drawing attention to the fact that our consciousness is the *medium* in which cognition occurs, while the conscious thinker in each of us is the actor on this stage, both as observer and knower, who makes sense of what appears *in* our consciousness. What is implied here is that all that we come to know as objects in the world *around and supposedly "outside"* us are in fact not separate from us, but rather are part of our general consciousness that embraces them, as a stage embraces the actors and objects that appear on it. I see this to be a very significant metaphor, the full meaning of which will become apparent in this and following Chapters. Steiner then goes on to summarize and add to what he earlier characterized as thinking and conceptual thought. He makes several points.

1. First, he states that we form or remember concepts as we think about our sense perceptions of the world. These perceptions do not themselves give us our concepts. We are given sense impressions through our eyes, ears, and so on, and each impression presents itself to us singly without revealing its meaning or its relation to other impressions that may accompany it, precede it, or follow it.

I describe the process to myself as follows: I may hear a noise, also see a movement, and observe a flying object landing on my arm, and feel a sensation on my skin, but these sense impressions do not *of themselves reveal* what they have to do with one another or with some object. What I come to know about them I do through thinking: "Ah, there is a mosquito in the room, I heard and saw it just now, it is the source of that sound, and here it is about to bite me." Thus I use my thinking and concepts to identify these impressions and to discover their interrelationships. Two common concepts that we often use to discover relationships are cause and effect. "That mosquito is the cause of my sensations." By means of such concepts, our thinking takes us above and beyond what our sense organs individually and separately report to us.

2. Secondly, Steiner argues that thinking is *not* what is often described as a subjective, personal activity. This is because thinking is what *determines* subjectivity and objectivity; these concepts are applied by thinking to structure our world. So thinking itself is neither subjective nor objective; it stands, as it were, above them or prior to them. As Steiner points out, "I should never say that my individual subject thinks; rather, it lives by the grace of thinking."[13] I find this to be an extremely important point, which he proceeds to explain.

Going on, Steiner writes that rather than being simply an individual's subjective act, thinking is a *universal* activity, meaning, I think, an activity in which *all* of us can and do take part and *by means of which* we identify ourselves and others, communicate to one another and relate ourselves to the world. Once I realize that what I conceive (or mean) by means of thinking, *you* can also think and understand, then it becomes clear that thinking is a common capacity and that concepts are by their nature universally accessible and intelligible. So my thinking, though it does go on in and through me, is equally accessible to you, as long as you make the effort in thinking to understand the concepts of which my thinking has made use.

3. Steiner's third point has to do with our sense impressions or *percepts,* as he names them. He and other philosophers agree that our percepts do not always reveal to us the way things actually are. As they put it, it is *naive* to assume the validity of our sense perceptions or that what we simply perceive gives us the full reality. For this reason, people who do believe that our percepts alone give us the full reality of what is perceived are referred to as *Naive Realists.* For example, assuming that someone whom we perceive to be angry *is* actually angry would be a naive assumption. To find out the truth we would need to inquire further and, through shared thoughts, determine what is actually the case.

---

13   Ibid., p. 53

Steiner points out two categories of perception: there are "mathematical"and "qualitative" percepts. Our perceived distance from objects and their perceived position in space is an example of the former; our perceptions of warmth, cold, the color spectrum, sounds and tones are examples of the latter. With our thinking we realize that these two categories of perception must be, initially at least, *subjective* in nature and open to error because they are dependent on our relative position in space and on the working of our sense organs. For example, we can be wrong about how far away we are from certain objects or about our perception of what we think of as a light source, for our eye does not always discriminate effectively. That is, the perception of light can be due not only to an actual source of light impinging on the eye, but also to a mechanical blow to the optic nerve. It was discovered in Steiner's time that no matter what stimulates the optic nerve, the perception of light is always the result.

4. Steiner's fourth point in this Chapter is equally important in its relation to the process of our cognizing the world. He refers to what many modern philosophers have concluded: there are definite *limits* pertaining to our knowledge of the world and its processes. Because of such discoveries concerning the functioning of our sense organs as mentioned above, philosophers were led to the conviction that our empirical knowledge of the world was necessarily subjective, that is, conditioned and altered by our sense organs, and that the nature of things as they are *in themselves* was therefore inaccessible to science. Steiner refers to the conclusions physiologists of his time had reached concerning the process of our visual perception of the world. Our optic nerves

> fundamentally alter the external impressions received by the eye....and what goes on in the brain is connected to the external process through so many intermediate processes that we cannot imagine any similarity between them....yet even these (processes) the soul does not perceive directly.

> What we ultimately have in consciousness are not brain processes at all, but *sensations* (ie., of color) and *mental pictures* somehow formed from what the sensory processes have transmitted."[14]

Such observations have led to the conclusion that a good part, if not all, of our knowledge of the world perceived through our senses is "subjective." "Hard" science has therefore sought to base our knowledge of the world on a limited number of physical phenomena that can be weighed and measured, the so-called "primary" qualities, which are judged to be accurate and "objective." Avoiding our unreliable sense organs, physics today envisions an atomic and subatomic world of particles and fields as the basis of matter, though we cannot perceive them directly but only the "traces" of them registered on electron microscopes. Physicists *infer* this underlying reality of things on the basis of experiments that could possibly represent or model that reality, and they describe the objects and activities of this world mathematically, ie., with little or no regard for sensory perception.

As a philosophical standpoint, Steiner and his contemporaries referred to this modern scientific approach as Critical Idealism, a term that implies that what our thinking can grasp of the *perceived* world is always going to be hypothetical or inferential rather than certain knowledge because of dissimilarities in and between the nature of our sense organs, the stages of nerve transmission, brain processes, and our actual sensations that we relate to an assumed independent reality outside ourselves. However, as Steiner now points out, if it is in fact the case that our knowledge of the world is hypothetical and inconclusive, then even this conclusion of the Critical Idealists must also itself be hypothetical and inconclusive. To claim that their view of the role of perception in cognition and its effect on our knowing is the truth of the matter is therefore self-contradictory.

Steiner ends this Chapter with the reflection that another way must be found to gain a trustworthy means of understanding the

---

14   Ibid., p. 65

role played by our percepts and concepts in the search for knowledge. The explanation and conclusions of the Critical Idealists fail to provide us with that understanding due to the assumptions and self-contradictory nature of their reasoning. If our search for knowledge cannot reach the realm of "things in themselves," but only infer it, it also cannot reach certainty in regard to the role played by our sense organs in cognition, for they too must belong to the realm of things in themselves. Therefore the assumed truth of Critical Idealism, that all sensory knowledge must be subjective, has no firm basis. Steiner will now seek another path to understanding the nature of our cognitive activity.

5. Knowing the World

In this next Chapter Steiner lays out in more detail what he has already referred to in Chapter 3, where he described the role thinking plays in grasping the nature of our percepts and their relationship to one another in the cognitive process.

1. First, though, he reviews once more the faulty reasoning of Critical Idealism by summarizing its view of the process of perception, beginning from an original percept of an object through its reception in the eye or some other sense organ, leading on through nerves to the brain and eventually into consciousness in the form of a sensation (hot, cold, hard, soft, etc.), a process in which, it assumes, the original percept goes through so many changes that the original is lost in the final one, and the object itself can only be thought of as a transcendent thing-in-itself, inaccessible to cognition. Therefore, such philosophers maintain, our knowledge of this and all sensed objects in general is in fact a subjective knowledge consisting only of the last step in the process, referred to as conscious sensations and mental pictures produced in the mind that are supposed to represent the objects of perception, but which cannot be known to accurately represent them as they are "in themselves," independent of our attempts to know them.

Once again, Steiner points out that the self-contradiction of Critical Idealism lies in the fact that its view of the whole process of sense perception must itself *also* be only a lot of mental pictures as the last step in a series of sense impressions, nerve transmissions, and brain operations, turning this whole edifice of thought into a hypothetical theory rather than being an objective truth concerning perception and cognition.

2. Steiner next reiterates his view that our activity of cognition proceeds according to our organization. We do not perceive a particular percept *for the first time* with full understanding of its nature and identity. When sensory percepts arise in our consciousness for the first time, we do not at once know what they are; we don't *recognize* them. Not until we think into such percepts can we arrive at a knowledge of what they really are. Through thinking, we then are able to intuit their nature and can refer to them as objects of knowledge. Perceiving and thinking are separate functions of our organization. Steiner suggests that there could be a being whose perceiving and thinking coincide, so that perceiving immediately renders understanding. For such a being, we could say that the percept and concept (or meaning) arise at once in perception; that being would immediately see the concept in or together with the percept. Imagining such a being helps us to understand that the concepts we intuit in thinking actually belong to or inform the percepts we experience in perceiving, although we do not perceive them that way initially because of the way we are organized.[15]

Steiner then describes our human situation, which makes each of us a "twofold creature" with two distinct features as perceivers and thinkers.

> "I am enclosed within the realm that I perceive as my personality, but I am also the bearer of an activity that determines my limited existence from a higher sphere. Our thinking, unlike our sensing and feeling, is not individual. It is universal. Only because it is related to the individual's feeling and

15 Steiner, ibid., p. 81

sensing does it receive an individual stamp in each separate human being. Human beings differentiate themselves from one another through these particular colorations of universal thinking.[16]

He made a similar characterization of our nature already in Chapter 3.

3. Returning to the view of perception of Critical Idealism, Steiner next points out that the whole process of sense perception from sense impressions, to nerve transmissions, to brain interpretations, to actual sensations, could *only* be considered objectively real and true by a Naive Realist or Critical Idealist, if it were in fact *perceived* in its entirety as a cause-effect *relationship* of events involving our sense organs, nerves, brain, and consciousness. But this relationship of individual events in the body and consciousness is *not perceivable* as a causal relationship, in this case one of causality from an external object impinging on our senses, then our nerves, brain, and consciousness. This relationship is only *thinkable* (or conceptually conceivable). And the assumed fact that the object perceived exists *independently of us*, complete in itself, is also not perceivable. It too is only conceivable and lacks actual, perceptual verification.

As Steiner has already indicated in Chapter 3, it is precisely the role of our thinking to *grasp the relationships* between and among individual percepts so as to understand *what* they are and *how* they relate or interact. The reality of all the objects of knowledge, and the objective world as a whole, consists in this *combination* of our percepts and concepts arrived at through thinking. The so-called "real" objective world cannot be known to exist *independently* of our perceiving and thinking, for we have no perception of such an existence. However, in Steiner's view, Critical Idealists seem not to have recognized this fact. They simply assume that reality as such *is* independent of our thinking and perceiving. But there is no way to prove this assumption, for in our experience there are *only* percepts and concepts of things. For us there is *nothing else* at hand that is verifiably

16   Ibid., p. 83

independent of these two elements. They, and only they, make up the nature and content of what we sense and think of as reality.[17]

Recognizing this fact, Steiner points out once again that thinking is an activity that takes hold of our sense perceptions and organizes them into conceptualized objects and their relationships. Every object of consciousness consists of certain sense perceptions unified by thinking into some kind of "thing." Similarly, our own being as a distinct person or subject is a concept arrived at by thinking about sense perceptions directed towards ourselves, which Steiner refers to as our self-percepts. Those sensed percepts that I identify in thinking as pertaining to something other than my perceived bodily self are categorized by thinking as "objective," in contrast to "subjective" self-percepts.

What, more specifically, are "subjective" percepts for Steiner? They are percepts of what we conceive of as our body and its conditions, and they are percepts of our feelings and sensations. We grasp them in their particularity by means of thinking, and we organize them, also by means of thinking, as elements of our personal nature. We define ourselves conceptually as subjects through such percepts and distinguish ourselves from others and the world through them, but we can only do so by means of thinking. Steiner also includes what he terms our "mental pictures" of objects as belonging to our subjectivity, because they are memory pictures retained by each person. They refer to experiences from the past.

4. In regard to the term "mental pictures" (*vorstellungen* in the original German), Steiner refers in this Chapter to the philosopher Schopenhauer, who considered thinking to be an "abstract" activity, consisting only of "mental pictures" rather than real things, a view that was espoused by many in his and in our time. Such pictures do not embody the reality of things. On the other hand, Schopenhauer maintained, we can only meet true *reality* through the direct, immediate experience, in perception, of our body and its activity as well as other bodies.[18] But Steiner points out that this sensory experience

17   Steiner, ibid., pp. 90-91
18   Ibid., page 87

of our body simply involves a series of percepts whose nature and interrelationships are only knowable through thinking and concept acquisition. Their *true* reality consists not only in what we can perceive of them but also in what we come to understand conceptually about them.

5. The last point I will mention from Chapter 5 concerns what Steiner says about concept acquisition. He indicates that we do not *form* concepts in the sense of building each one up ourselves, but we rather *intuit* them.[19] Concepts, and their more complex form as ideas, come to (or appear to) us as objects of intellectual intuition. I recall from my studies of ancient Greek that this characterization corresponds with the ancient Greek use of the word for an "idea," which meant something actually seen, not with our physical eyes, but with the inner eye of understanding. Intuition involves the "ahha" experience of grasping or understanding something for the first time. A simple example would be my experience of discerning shapes and shadows, while walking with my wife in the woods at night, without a flashlight. These shapes were at first just individual percepts whose nature and relationship we could not fathom in the darkness. Gradually, we knit some of them into a shape we identified conceptually as an animal, whose additional feature, a lighter shadow paler than the rest of him, gave us the final intuition (or concept): it's a skunk!

Someone might object to this way of describing that insight. He might argue that we simply *remembered the shape and name* of the thing before us. We recognized the shape before us as an animal of some kind and then recalled a mental picture of a skunk which we had encountered before in nature or in a book. Our so-called intuition was nothing more than the name of a memory of the animal previously experienced and learned. However, this name is not something arbitrary, a word that was at one time simply assigned to an animal of that kind. It bears *within it* a range of *meanings* based on the perceived characteristics of skunks. Such meanings are what

---

19   Ibid., page 88

concepts refer to. They are what make the skunk intelligible to us as a kind of animal, just as the concept of animal expresses the meaning (or nature) of that kind of thing, as compared to a plant or stone.

In our intuition of the skunk, we were not simply engaged with a memory picture of its shape and with a name for it, we were "seeing into" the very nature of the thing before us—in other words, its concept. Thus, the concepts of things actually and in reality belong to them and are not merely subjective interpretations. We cognize them in things as belonging to them. Of course, our cognition may not be complete and can even be a case of mistaken identity, but that can be corrected with more precise observation and thought.

When children learn the names of things, they do not at first understand the conceptual content referred to by those names. To do so, their thinking must awaken and by its means they can come to understand what a skunk really is in the fullness of its nature. Simply looking at a skunk over and over again will not yield that understanding. Thinking must also be awakened to discover the full meaning of being skunk. Of course, there are people who are content with the name of a thing and do not seek to know anything more about it by thinking into the full range of its percepts.

Simply put, Steiner's epistemological insight is this: every object we encounter has its concept "within" it as its nature. Our thinking enables us to "see" this concept when we observe with our senses, identifying our percepts and their interconnections by using our thinking. Thereby, the object's functioning and its various characteristics, both mathematical and qualitative (see my summary of Chapter 3) come to light for us as the full concept, or identity, of the thing. To say that our concept is merely a name arbitrarily assigned to that object (as the Nominalists did in the Middle Ages), ignores the depth of observation and thinking that belongs to it. Yes, in one respect, the name is arbitrary, only because other words in other languages were chosen and are also used in referring to it. What is a name, after all, but the verbal clothing assigned to what has been discovered through observation and thinking by a specific language group. Concepts, unlike names, are not simply assigned to things.

They present, and then represent, the intelligible, ideal nature of things.

Of course, the range of meaning of any object conceived by our thinking depends on the range of our observation of it, that is, of the kind and quality of our percepts. Our modern view of the solar system replaced the view and understanding of medieval civilization. Further observations of the stars are now leading to a far more complex system involving the revolving and rotating movements within and among galaxies, to mention just one aspect. So our worldview is again being reformulated, as a result of new and deeper levels of understanding of what is in fact "out there" for us to observe and think into, seeking further intuitions, as we expand the field of our thinking consciousness.

By now in this summary of Steiner's epistemology I have described what for him are the basic elements of cognition. *Percepts* are the data provided by our sense organs, which appear to us initially as unidentified in themselves and unrelated to each other. *Concepts* (and ideas) are intuitions by which we understand the meaning and nature of percepts and their relationships to each other. *Objective concepts* are the intelligible element of those things we have identified (through thinking) as being separate from our bodily selves. Concepts by which we identify our *bodies, feelings, and memories (mental pictures)* pertain to our being as subjects, distinct from objects, and so may be called *subjective concepts*, also identified in and by means of our universal, thinking consciousness.

Our cognitive activity involves all of the above. It recognizes that for humans there is no external, "real" world that is *independent* of cognition, existing in and by itself and impinging on our senses. The world's reality, of which we are a part, consists of the full range of percepts of which we are, have been or will be conscious. It also consists of the full range of concepts that we intuit as belonging to those percepts as their meanings, identity, interrelationships, and laws of being. In other words, the world we perceive and know lies *within* our thinking consciousness, which *embraces* both the world and our bodily separation from it as individual thinkers. Do we each inhabit the same world? Our percepts may vary from one person to the next, but our thoughts are accessible to all thinkers. Out of them we build our common world, or fail to.

6. Human Individuality

1. By way of review, Steiner begins Chapter 6 with a further clarification of the term "mental pictures." He has already described them as memories of things we have encountered. More specifically, he now describes them as consisting of a memory picture of a percept that we have united with its concept through thinking. Thus, it is an "individualized concept" as it has a specific perceptual reference.[20] Let us say that a percept is observed and its concept (identity) is then intuited and grasped. Example: "Hmm, what is that? I'll look closer. Ah, it must be a can opener." What remains in consciousness *afterwards* is the memory or mental picture of that *particular* can opener, which I identified by means of the *general* concept "can opener." In other words, my memory or mental picture of a can opener involves or combines both a concrete percept and its *conceived*, conceptual identity.

Steiner describes our mental pictures as "subjective" in nature, because we form and store them in our individual minds. Another example: We see a piece of furniture with an unusual shape and construction. At first we are not sure what it is supposed to be. We are able to identify it as a table by means of that concept whose meaning might be expressed as follows: "a flat surface on which to place things with some means of support off the ground." That particular table with its specific form and its concept (involving its function or purpose) is now within us as a mental picture, for as long as we remember it.

However, the "subjectivity" of our mental pictures *does not imply that we have only a subjective knowledge of the table.* Once again, Steiner

---

20 Steiner, ibid., p. 100

explains that dualistic philosophers have concluded that our knowledge is subjective because 1) our mental pictures are formed from the percepts acquired by means of our sense organs, and 2) our sensory system along with our bodies are separate from the assumed-as-independent-of-our-thinking, perceived world and only give us an impression of that world of things which is produced, filtered and altered by the complexity of our sensory processes in the nerves and brain. These conclusions have led them to the idea that the actual nature of things is inaccessible to us. A naive person may think that his or her perception of a tree is accurate, but, for the Dualist or Critical Idealist, it is not. All he can say is that our knowledge of the actual object is limited to and by what our senses and resulting sensations tell us. What the tree is "in itself" we cannot perceive and know.

In previous Chapters, Steiner has already referred to the mistake such philosophers make in assuming the independent existence of "things in themselves." All we have to go on in our experience of the world are percepts and concepts. For us humans, the "world" can be known and understood only by means of them. Thinkers who claim the existence of a "world-in-itself" contradict themselves. They think they know the existence of what they think cannot be known.

Steiner uses a peculiar phrase to describe our all-embracing cognitive activity. He terms it the "universal world process."[21] In Chapters 3 and 5 he describes it as a *two-stage* process of our consciousness *in and by means of which* the world, or the universe, appears (or is given) to us and then comes to be known. The first stage is perceptual, during which the world appears in consciousness as a manifold of unrelated percepts. In the second stage, the conceptual meaning and interrelationships of those precepts is intuited through thinking. Thinking brings about the second stage: it enables the (gradual) cognition of the contents, relationships, and the overall structure of the whole universe. Thus we are able to move from the initial, puzzling *appearance* of the world in perception to what, for us, becomes

---

21   Steiner, ibid., pp. 97-98, 102

and is its *reality* in thinking. This is not to say that what we conceive of as reality at present is the full truth. We may gain access to further percepts and concepts by means of which our view of reality is altered or expanded.

As thinkers and knowers we are more than our perceived, individual, bodily selves. As thinkers we embody this second stage of the "universal world process," which works through us, or more precisely, through our thinking. For Steiner, the "universal world process" is a process of human perceiving and thinking consciousness *in which* the manifold contents of the universe first appear to us and are then understood. This, at least, is my interpretation of what he means by the term, for he does not spell it out. He seems to leave it to the reader to figure it out, thus engaging our thinking!

2. Ending this review, Steiner goes on to describe the nature of our *individuality*. If we were only cognitive beings, we would simply be gatherers of knowledge about the world with no particular individual *preferences*. We *individuate* by means of our feelings, which express our particular preferences. For example, feelings of pleasure or pain express our individual responses and reactions to our experiences. In Chapter 3 Steiner described our dual nature as humans. There he indicated that our thinking both unites us with things by understanding their conceptual nature, while at the same time it distinguishes us from them through our identification with our bodies. Thus our dual nature includes our bodily *individuality* and our conceptual *universality* as thinkers. Here in Chapter 6 he states that, in addition to our bodies, our feelings and emotions also serve to identify and individuate us from others.

Feelings are qualitative percepts that we experience inwardly and come to know conceptually. As pure percepts, only I can experience my own feelings. Once known and described conceptually, my feelings become accessible to the thinking of others and empathy becomes possible, which is a further feeling. But to say, "I understand how you are feeling" does not imply that I experience a feeling exactly the same way as you do, for it is impossible to know whether my particular feeling is the same as yours. Words, concepts, can only grasp in a generic way what someone else is actually feeling without being able to convey exactly his or her actual percept of the feeling itself.

Everyone knows what it is like to experience strong feelings that seem to overwhelm or confuse us. To get to the point where I can say, "I *understand* what I am feeling," on the other hand, makes it possible for me (and you) to gain some distance from the grip of feelings so that they do not overpower me. Thinking makes this possible.

3. Steiner goes on to characterize people in terms of those who live more in their feelings, those who live more in their thoughts and those who achieve a balance of feeling and thinking. A person who achieves this balance he terms a "true individual." Because of this balance, they are able, as he puts it, to "reach the highest with their feelings into the region of ideals." That is, true individuals are able to unite their feeling life with their thinking in forming ideals for their lives.[22]

What is an ideal? It is a conceived value (a concept) that we respect, even love, and *want* to realize in life through our own efforts, our own will. Perhaps it is an ideal way of living, or an ideal manner of relating to others, or a particular ability that we respect and aspire to develop. We will find in the second part of Steiner's *Philosophy of Freedom* that this "feeling for ideals" is a key element in achieving freely willed actions in life.

7. Are There Limits to Knowledge?

In this next Chapter Rudolf Steiner returns once again to the central theme of the first part of his book: epistemology or the theory of knowledge. He once again addresses the difference between his Monism and the Dualism of many of his contemporaries. He defends his point of view by pointing to the contradictions in the Dualist outlook. The reader will know by now Steiner's theory and the manner in which he again defends it. Our knowing consists of two elements: percepts and concepts, by means of which we are able both to

---

observe the world and comprehend it. He summarizes the cognitive process as follows:

> Let us call the way in which the world meets us, before it has gained its true form through cognition, "the world of appearance," in contrast to the unified reality composed of percepts and concepts. We can then say that the world is given to us as a duality, and cognition assimilates it into a (monistic) unity. A philosophy that proceeds from this fundamental principle can be characterized as monistic philosophy or *monism*. In contrast to it stands two-world theory or *dualism*. The latter does not assume that there are two sides to a unitary reality that are separated merely by our organization, but that there are two worlds that are absolutely distinct from one another.[23]

For Steiner, as we have seen, our knowledge of the nature of things (objects) and their interrelationships is made up of their perceptual content, their concepts, and the conceptual relations and laws governing them. On the other hand, Dualists believe that

> "the whole world would evaporate into an abstract conceptual schema if "real" connections were not affirmed alongside the conceptual connections of objects. In other words, the conceptual principles discoverable through thinking appear too airy to Dualists, and so they look for additional, real principles by which to support them."[24]

Having stated this, Steiner now sets out to investigate what Dualists mean by such "real principles." He refers first to Naive Realism, the philosophical position that only our sense perceptions

---

23   Ibid., p. 104
24   Steiner, ibid., p. 110

constitute the reality of things. Our thinking and concepts add nothing real to our experience. For example, "the idea of a tulip counts only as an abstraction, as an unreal thought image that the soul assembles from characteristics common to all tulips."[25] Only the actual tulip before my eyes is the real thing. However, Steiner points out that our experience contradicts this, for that tulip passes away and only the species tulip, or kind, endures. The species must be the real thing. Naive realism cannot accept such an idea (or generality), as real, and simply accepts the transient nature of things. Or, being unsatisfied with this, seeks instead to base the reality of things on something perceptual that endures.

Today, for example, we look for concrete percepts of what endures in a tulip, and all other plants and living things, and we think we have found it in their genes. We think that the real tulip is produced by genetic strands of DNA and RNA consisting of elements which constitute the tulip's genetic code and which, in turn, govern the formation, growth and reproduction of the cells that compose a tulip. Individual plants die but their genetic code endures in their seeds, bulbs, or corms and brings about new cellular growth from there. To the questions, "How does a gene actually bring about reproduction of cells?, or "How does it translate its code of instructions into an actual life process?," the so-called "naive" answer might be, "Through observed chemical reactions." To the question, "What causes such reactions?," some have answered, "We don't know yet" while others have said, "We think that within the plant there is a life force that acts by means of the genetic code and attendant chemical reactions." In the latter case, Steiner would claim that the Naive Realist has become a Metaphysical Realist, for the latter now proposes the existence of an *unperceived* life force that somehow expresses itself through the genetic code of individual plants.[26]

---

25 Ibid., p. 113

26 Steiner himself spoke of the existence of the life force in living things, which he termed the etheric body. However, he actually perceived this force at work, while many today have simply inferred its presence as I mention here and so may be termed metaphysical realists, for they lack the actual percept of that force.

At this point in the Chapter, Steiner refers to Metaphysical Realism as "a contradictory mixture of Naive Realism and Idealism, whose hypothetical forces (like the supposed life force) are imperceptible entities with perceptual qualities."[27] In Steiner's example of the tulip, which I have embellished above by referencing genetic research, a supposed Metaphysical Realist has attempted to grasp the true abiding nature of the tulip by means of the concept of a life force, which is thought of along the lines of a real, *perceivable* physical force, but which *cannot be perceived* as such.

This is the contradiction to which Steiner here refers: it is an abstract idea, without having any actual, perceptible content itself. There is only the impermanent plant that supposedly provides "perceptual qualities" of that force, although we cannot perceive the life force *itself* in them. We can only assume its presence. Whereas for Steiner, it is sufficient to say that the tulip's nature is a combination of our percepts of it and our conceptual understanding of them, including the genetic material observed and conceived of in more recent times, without such unperceivable assumptions as a life force. We don't need a concept like the life force to explain the physical reality of a tulip unless, that is, *we can actually perceive it* and then relate it to the other observed phenomena of the tulip. The species concept and its expression in a genetic code is sufficient, at least for what we can perceive as physical reality. It is not an abstract concept applied to tulips, it is the very nature that unites the various qualities that we perceive in a tulip and that endures.

> "We must admit that the *relationships* between percepts, as transmitted through thinking, can have no other form of existence for us than that of concepts. If we reject the invalid components of metaphysical realism, the world presents itself as the sum of percepts and their conceptual (ideal) relations.... The worldview into which metaphysical realism merges when it eliminates its contradictory elements can

---

27   In his later writings and lectures," Ibid., p. 115

be called monism, because it combines one-sided realism with idealism in a higher unity."[28]

This "higher unity" to which Steiner refers here is, I think, what results when concepts are recognized to be the intelligible nature of our percepts rather than abstract ideas which our thinking then applies to perception. Thinking makes sense of our perceptions by discovering the conceptual meaning *in them*. The meaning and significance of any concept, its full reality, is given in the percepts which it (the concept) identifies. Concepts are only valid and not abstract when they have actual percepts as their content.

The life force supposed or imagined by Metaphysical Realists in the example above has no actual perceptual content; for them. It is thought to exist invisibly behind or within our perceptions of what it animates. For Steiner, it is therefore an invalid concept and provides us with no actual knowledge. For the so-called life force to be a real object of knowledge, it must have a perceptual content, that is, we must be able to perceive it itself. Until we humans develop the capacity for actually perceiving the life force at work, reference to it is not admissible in Steiner's view.

Steiner's Monism sets no absolute limits to our knowing. We are only limited by the extent of our perceptions and our thoughts about them. That is a relative and not an absolute limitation. Monists recognize that understanding the world depends on our uniting our perceptions with concepts that identify and explain them. Monists start from perceptions and seek their concepts. But they can also start from concepts like the life force and seek the percepts of them. This requires that they cultivate their senses, learning to see, hear, touch, etc. more sensitively. They must develop more refined, "higher" senses. Their field of thinking consciousness then will fill with more contents arising through more sensitive doors of perception.

What I have written above is my summation of what I take to be the essential content of this Chapter, "Are There Limits to Knowledge?" Steiner sums it up in the following words:

---

28   Ibid., p. 115-116

Our cognition involves questions that emerge for us because a conceptual sphere, pointing to the totality of the world, confronts a perceptual sphere conditioned by place, time, and subjective organization. Our task is to balance these two spheres, both of which we know well. This has nothing to do with a limit to cognition. At a particular time, this or that might remain unexplained because the place of our vantage point in life prevents us from perceiving the things in question. But what is not found today may be found tomorrow. The limits determined in this way are only temporary, and they can be overcome by progress in perception and thinking.[29]

I have now reached the end of Part I of Steiner's book, which he titled *The Knowledge of Freedom*. In this part of the book, Steiner has presented the reader with four significant facts about thinking and cognition.

First, he has shown how we come to know the world, through sensory observation and conceptual, intuitive thinking. We have no other means of knowing the reality of the sensory world than this. For us as humans, the reality of all things and events consists in the combination of our perceptions of them with their concepts, or meanings and significance, intuited in thinking.

Second, he has argued that there can be no absolute limits to our cognizing the world as long as we agree with the first fact.

Third, he has indicated how, through introspection, we can discover that we are *free in the activity of thinking and cognizing*, it being our own *self-produced and self-sustaining activity*. This fact, together with the Monist view that there are no absolute limits to cognition, explain to me Steiner's choice of the title of this part of his book: *The*

---

29   Steiner, ibid., p. 108-109

Knowledge of Freedom. This knowledge is *unlimited* in its reach, and as a process of thinking is itself our own self-induced, and therefore free, spiritual activity.

Fourth, once we have affirmed the truth that thinking is a free and self-sustaining activity, which, as Steiner points out in Chapter 3, is not normally observed, then we cannot subscribe to the view that the brain thinks in us. Though we can observe neural brain activity when thinking occurs (an activity connected with our sense organs and nerves and with thinking itself), we know that such neural activity is not itself causing and sustaining our thinking as we engage in it. We can perceive ourselves doing it through our own effort to think and understand. The thinker in each of us is the free and self-active one, which Steiner calls our spirit.

Next, in Part 2 of the book, Steiner goes on to show how we can be free in our practical activity in the world, or, to put it in other words, how we can achieve free will in realizing our goals in practical life.

PART II

The Reality of Freedom

8: *The Factors of Life*

Steiner begins Chapter 8 with another summary of the process of cognition as described in Part I of his book. He once again reviews the elements of cognition: percepts, concepts, and our power of thinking that discerns, identifies, and relates concepts and percepts together. Then he refers to the fact that we are not only cognitive beings. Together with thinking, we experience *feelings* and we exert our *will* in our actions in accord with our aims and our motivations. Thus we are three-fold beings; these three components of our being are the factors of life which he now addresses.

For Steiner, these three factors have an *equal* importance and significance for human life. However, for many people only one of them is the predominant factor in our self-experience. He points out that for some, that factor is feeling, while for others it is willing. Such people have not realized the essential role played by thinking in our experience of feeling and willing. They assign to thinking a subordinate status. It is something we do that merely reflects the actual reality of our feeling and willing activity in life, which it captures in memory. In our thinking we only have an indirect, remembered experience of life or simply a series of abstract thoughts. In feeling and willing, on the other hand, we connect directly with the world.

Steiner asserts that people who assign this special status to feeling or willing are Naive Realists. That is, they take their immediate perceptual experience in feeling or will activity as true reality. Earlier, in Chapter 4, Steiner associated the term Naive Realism with the conviction that our perceptions alone give us the full reality of the world. As we have seen, this sense of reality is naive, for the following reason. Without the thinking that accompanies our perceiving, we are left with an unrelated sequence of percepts whose identity and relation to one another is unknown. For example, feeling-percepts do not yield knowledge, or understanding. We perceive that we are feeling something, within us or there before us, without at first knowing what it is. We then seek the thoughts that identify our feeling and explain its occurrence. Hence, thinking is equally important to feeling as a factor in our lives.

Steiner describes people who emphasize the role of feelings as follows:

> They try to make feeling, not knowing, the means of cognition. Since feeling is something altogether individual, something equivalent to perception, philosophers of feeling make something that has significance only within their own personality into the principle of the universe. They try to permeate the entire universe with their own selves. What *monism*, as described in this book, attempts to grasp conceptually, the philosophers of feeling seek to achieve with feeling. They see that kind of connection with things as more immediate.[30]

He refers to mysticism as an example of this orientation to life through feeling alone. There are indeed mystics who claim to have a feeling of God, of a supernatural presence touching their feelings. One might well ask of them, "Did you *know* for sure that God was with you? Maybe you imagined it." Others base their decisions in life

---

30   Steiner, ibid., p. 129

on feelings. "I did it because it *felt* right to me." Of them one might well ask, "But how did you *know* it was right, on what basis can you put so much trust in your feelings?" These questions call for other kinds of perceptions and their attendant thoughts which depend on thinking. "Did you *see* God or *hear* Him/Her?" "What gave you that feeling of rightness? Was it a previous experience?" But, often as not, people who depend on feelings experience them so strongly that their feelings themselves are persuasive. There are no doubts. Further questioning is irrelevant. "I just felt God's arms holding me." "I just felt in my gut that it was the right thing to do." For such people, thinking and thoughts are too general, they do not capture the immediacy and power of feeling, so that feeling is always going to be the most reliable factor in life. In feeling they feel most alive.

Proponents of the primacy of willing, of personal action in life, might say something similar: "I feel most alive when I am busily engaged in my projects." Philosophers of the Will, like Schopenhauer, go so far as to claim that in will activity we participate in the driving forces that have created and that sustain the universe. Such a person might say, "The creative powers live in me and I in them, and that is why, in being active, I am most alive."

Steiner states again that both kinds of Naive Realism which he has described here share the opinion that their immediate, direct experiences of feeling or willing are more *real* than thinking and thought. Steiner then points out that both the activity of willing and the surge of feelings remain simple, unconnected percepts in the field of consciousness until thinking takes hold of them, intuits their meaning and significance, and relates them to the rest of experience. But for the Naive Realist, convinced that the sense perceptions of feelings and willful impulses alone provide him or her with the full richness of life, I think it would be difficult to be persuaded by Steiner's presentation of the matter.

Steiner included an addendum to this short Chapter in a second edition of the book. He obviously wanted to inform the reader who is sympathetic with the standpoint of Naive Realism that one *can* nevertheless achieve an experience of thinking as something *even more real* than feeling or willing alone. I quote from this addition to the chapter:

> No other activity of the human soul is as easily mis-understood as thinking. Feeling and willing warm the human soul even when we look back and recollect their original state, while thinking all too easily leaves us cold. It seems to dry out the life of the soul. Yet this is only the sharply contoured shadow of the reality of thinking—a reality interwoven with light, dipping down warmly into the phenomena of the world. This dipping down occurs with a power that flows forth in the activity of thinking itself—the power of love in spiritual form.[31]

From this statement we can gather that Steiner experiences thinking as imbued with loving attention as he ponders "the phenomena of the world." Steiner points here to the possibility that everyone can experience this love-imbued activity of thinking. He states that a thinker who is capable of it will then experience *both* feeling and willing in his or her thinking, "both of these in the depths of their reality." The reader will discover, in the next Chapter of the book, that for Steiner this love-imbued power of intuitive thinking is a key to the achievement of free will.

9. The Idea of Freedom

In this Chapter, Steiner develops his idea of free will and presents the conditions for achieving it. It is a long and complex Chapter with many key terms to keep in mind. For that reason I have set some of those key terms as titles for each point he makes in developing the Chapter. He begins with another brief review.

---

31   Ibid., p. 133

PERCEIVING AND COGNIZING: A REVIEW

Steiner recalls once again the cognitive process. When we come to know a particular tree, first we gain percepts of it to which we then add concepts from our store of knowledge or directly from intuition. Thus, in cognizing, concepts follow upon the sensing of percepts. But this fact does not imply that it is merely a subjective decision to unite a particular concept with a percept. In other words, it is not an arbitrary association. He describes it thus: "The percept's connection with its concept is recognized *after* the act of perception; but their belonging together is determined by the situation itself." My example: If I decide that I am looking at an oak tree, I have assigned the concept "oak tree" with all that it involves, to *this* object because of various percepts I have of it, including, for example, the shape of its leaves, the form of its trunk, and the texture of its bark. Indeed, I have already differentiated it *as a tree* from its surroundings, using my thinking. Thus the "situation" as a whole helps me determine that it is an oak.

PERCEIVING OUR THINKING

Next, Steiner contrasts this cognitive process as just described with our cognition of thinking itself. While we intuit and combine concepts with our percepts each time we cognize (or re-cognize) an object in our perceptual field, this sequence of *distinct* activities (perceiving and thinking) does *not* occur when we perceive our thinking itself. For in that case, he writes, our perceiving and thinking, percepts and concepts, *coincide*.[32] In making this statement, Steiner then leaves it to the reader to understand and confirm it.

What does he mean by this "coincidence"? It is evident that the percept of our thinking process is not something *given* to us, as is the case with sense perceptions given to us via our sense organs. Rather, we can perceive our thinking *as we are doing it*, in the process of bringing forth, relating, and understanding thoughts. Active thinking is not given to us as sense impressions are, nor does it simply

---

32   Steiner, ibid., p. 136, paragraph 3

arise in our awareness, like percepts do; we *do* the thinking, we give it to ourselves, as it were. Active thinking can sense itself; it is its *own* sense organ.

Thus, we can perceive thinking as *we* bring it forth. Perceiving our thinking is a non-sensuous, non-physical experience. There is no sensory or physical intermediary; perceiving and thinking "coincide." Steiner calls it a spiritual perceiving, a spiritual experience in which the knower and the known are united and in relation to each other, a self-relation. He describes it thus:

> To observe thinking is to live, during the obser-
> vation, immediately within the weaving of a self-
> supporting spiritual entity. We could even say that
> whoever wants to grasp the essence of the spirit in
> the form in which it *first* presents itself to human
> beings can do so in the self-sustaining activity of
> thinking.[33]

Steiner then reminds us that when we are able to observe our own thinking, we experience an activity that is full of content: our thoughts. And he observes that these thoughts are not merely a "shadowy copy" of some object that we form in the mind, as many believe. That may be true of the mental pictures (or images) of objects that we harbor in our minds, but it is not true of pure concepts. They are full of their own intrinsic meanings. Rather than being "shadows" of things, they are the ideal or conceptual substantiality of things, without which there could *be* no things for us.

It is understandably difficult for us to comprehend what Steiner is claiming here. We experience our thinking and our thoughts as being generated by ourselves in our minds. How then could our thoughts be the substantiality of objects external to us, as present *in them* as they are "in our heads"? As he pointed out in Part 1 of the book, Steiner's Monistic point of view regards our thinking and our perceptions of objects as taking place *within* consciousness. As

---

33   Steiner, ibid., p. 136

we have seen, he disagrees with Dualists who maintain a fundamental, unbridgeable separation between our conscious subjectivity and the objects we encounter. The known entities we call subjects and objects, consisting of their percepts and concepts, exist together, in fact *come to be* for us, within thinking consciousness.

But it is our thinking that also separates us from objects by taking note of our bodily self-percept, while at the same time it unites us with them by grasping their being and nature as objects in thought. This may seem like mere subjective idealism, all of it taking place in the thinking mind. But the fact is—it all happens within human consciousness. Or, to put it differently, human consciousness *embraces* all that we know. We cannot know anything that may exist outside of consciousness, so how can we assume it exists there at all? As Steiner puts it, that would be "philosophizing into thin air."

THE PRONOUN "I" REFERS TO OUR THINKING SELF

The next point that Steiner makes concerns our use of the pronoun "I". As I mentioned in the summary of Chapter 2, there Steiner uses it to refer to the thinker in each of us, rather than to our bodies and feelings. As such it refers to our spiritual nature, for thinking is itself spiritual in nature, rather than being a physical process of the brain, as Steiner also claimed earlier. For Steiner, the term "spirit" refers (at least) to our non-material power to think. This power is our spiritual Self in action or manifestation, our "I" being.

For readers who are convinced that thinking is brought about by the brain, Steiner now adds parenthetically that a careful observation of thinking will reveal that, in fact, thinking causes brain activity to be "repressed" so that it (thinking) can operate freely. I think he may be referring here to the suppression of that brain activity brought about by our sense organs, a neural activity that produces our sensations. When we are actively thinking, such sensations and neural activity may well be repressed. Steiner does not indicate how we can gain such "a careful observation" of the brain. Perhaps our modern brain scanning devices can be of service here.

Further, he states that when we are actively thinking, any physical brain activity that we still might observe is in fact the result of our thinking and not the cause of it, like footprints left in sand.[34] This statement may well be supported by contemporary observations of changes in brain wave patterns that occur when, for example, thinkers meditate on a series of thoughts, images, or mental sounds.

THE DIFFERENCE BETWEEN THE
"I" AND "I CONSCIOUSNESS"

Steiner next differentiates between our thinking "I" and what he terms our "I Consciousness," which includes not just our thinking but our bodily perceptions, our feelings, beliefs, temperament, and our preferred activities of will. In other words, Steiner's use of the term "I Consciousness" refers to all of my personal identity.

He then proceeds to analyze that aspect of "I Consciousness" that has to do specifically with personal volition, which is the main theme of the Chapter. I will now summarize the essential elements that Steiner presents in his analysis of human willing and the development needed to achieve a truly free will.

THE BASIC COMPONENTS OF THE WILL:
MOTIVE AND MOTIVE POWER

Agreeing with philosophical tradition, Steiner indicates that there are two basic components of any act of will: a "motive" (or aim) and the "motive power" (or motivation) to achieve that motive. He then defines motives as "momentary determining principles of willing," while motive power is the "abiding determining principle of the individual." In other words, at any particular time, there will be a specific *motive, or aim,* for every action I undertake. But my *motive power* enabling me to act will be based on my "enduring character," or, as Steiner now adds, on my "characterological disposition."[35] However, he also adds that our characterological disposition can also affect

---

34 Steiner, ibid., pp. 137-8
35 Steiner, ibid., p. 139

which motives we choose for our actions. As we shall see, it is primarily one's characterological disposition that requires development if one is to achieve free willing.

CHARACTEROLOGICAL INFLUENCES BEHIND MOTIVES AND MOTIVE POWERS

Steiner now adds that a person's *motive powers* consist of the *feelings and impulses* that one experiences inwardly in life, while one's specific *motives or aims of action* are formed from one's store of mental pictures, or images, of people, things and events in the world with which one has formed a personal connection.[36] These mental pictures sum up for us our personal experience of the world.[37]

Thus our charactcrology affects both the aims we choose in life and our motivations to realise them. Example: In my early twenties, I chose to become a teacher. That was my general aim and the question was, at what level would I best want to teach? Based on my experience in graduate school, I opted for primary and secondary education. At that point my specific aim was to find a pedagogical method that was rich in art and movement, for I believed that such a method would serve children the best. And my motive power to act on that specific motive consisted of my strong feeling of sympathy for children and for all things artistic. Both my motivation and my motive were aspects of my characterology at that time.

MOTIVE POWER IN RELATION TO "LEVELS OF HUMAN LIFE"

Steiner next proceeds to describe in a general way various possible *motive powers*, based on a person's character, which will drive (or motivate) him to act. He identifies these powers in relation to "the elements that compose an individual life." These "elements" he describes as "levels" or "spheres" of human life. The first level he calls our *perceiving* (or sense perception), the second our *feeling life*,

---

36   The German word for mental picture is Vorstellung: an image held in and before the mind or mind's eye.

37   Ibid., pp. 140-141

while the third includes our *thinking and mental picturing, or remembering.* The fourth and final level of life, he terms our "*conceptual thinking without reference to a specific perceptual content.*"38 In other words, that level does not involve mental pictures, that is, images from past experience. Rather, as we shall see, it involves "moral intuitions" of what does not yet exist.

Steiner describes a person's possible motive powers in relation to each of these four levels upon which we lead our lives. The implication is that individuals and their motivations will differ depending on which level of life they tend most to live. A further implication is that these are *levels or stages on the path of personal development*, for, in what follows, Steiner states that the final level of conceptual thinking is the "highest" level, a term which implies development. At this point in the text, he presents these levels quite objectively without an analysis of what I would call their "free will potential." In listing them below, I have also commented on that potential, indicating whether actions based on them would be free or not.

1. FIRST LEVEL OF HUMAN LIFE: SENSE PERCEPTION

There are two motive powers of the will that he puts on the first level of Perceiving: Drives and Social Tact. From what Steiner describes of them, it seems clear to me he is referring to times when one is living and acting exclusively on this first level of human life. One is not engaged at the same time on the other three levels of life, which could, but in this case do not, influence one's actions.

1A. PERCEPTIONS WHICH STIMULATE NATURAL DRIVES

The first motive power on the level of our perceiving Steiner identifies as our natural *drives* (that we *perceive* arising from our bodies and organic functions.) They tend to be immediate responses to perceptions. He identifies two *drives*: hunger and sexual desire. When we perceive our hunger pangs or a sexual stimulation in our

---

38 Steiner, ibid., p. 141 ff.

physical organization, we are at once motivated by these perceptions to seek food or sexual satisfaction.

1B. PERCEPTIONS WHICH RESULT
IN TACTFUL RESPONSES

The second motive power, which arises on this first, perceptual level of experience, consists of our immediate, *tactful responses* to situations that we perceive in our surroundings. These refer to our habitual reactions based on conventional social behavior in which we have been trained during our upbringing. Examples might include the immediate, automatic shaking of hands, giving up a seat on a bus, saying "please" and "thank you," deferring to elders and so on.

Both of these motive powers generally operate in us as inducements to act *without deliberation*. That is, influences from the spheres of feeling or mental picturing or pure thinking do not operate here. I think that is why he characterizes these motive powers as "immediate" responses to what we perceive. On the path of personal development towards free will, these actions are not themselves free, for they are motivated by natural instincts or by habit and ingrained behavior patterns. That is, I am not acting freely as a thinker if an instinct or a habit *alone* moves me to act. Steiner does not say this at this point in the Chapter; he seems to leave it up to the reader to reach his or her own conclusion.

2. SECOND LEVEL: FEELING—MOTIVE
POWERS AS SPECIFIC FEELINGS

Next, Steiner indicates how feeling (or emotion), the second level of our life, can become a motive power inducing us to act. For example, a feeling of compassion may arise in us in response to our perceptions of people in need and lead us to help in some way. He lists a number of feelings such as remorse, anger, gratitude, loyalty, love and duty which can operate in us as motive powers. Again, the reader may wonder if such motivation, based on feeling, enables free will. To me, it does not seem to be a sufficient condition for free action.

That is because feelings alone can often cause me to act impulsively without actually understanding the situation before me. Without understanding, I (as a thinker) am not fully in charge of my action.

3. THIRD LEVEL: MENTAL PICTURES— MOTIVE POWERS BASED ON MEMORY

The third level of our life consists of our thinking *in relation to our life experiences* stored in memory. The kind of thinking involved here focuses on our mental images, or memories, from our past. Our thinking motivates us to act based on these recollections. For example, my coming upon someone working on his car may bring up a memory of my own experience of making a similar repair of my car, and this would be an inducement to get involved and help him with his. Similarly, remembering the rules and procedures of first aid can be the incentive for choosing a certain kind and manner of bandaging a wound. Or the memory of a certain behavior or moral precept which we have been taught, like opening a door for an elder, will motivate us to do just that. Such memories form what Steiner and others have called our fund of "practical experience."

Can such actions motivated by memories from the past be called free actions? I will answer "yes, but not entirely." Yes, my memory image from the past, in effect, tells me what to do, and I freely decide to go along with it. No, not entirely free, because I (as thinker) have not come up with my action appropriate for *this* occasion as an original insight, gained *in the present*. I am guided by past experience rather than present-time thinking and discovery. Living solely on the basis of past experience and past learning, one is not free in the present to intuit, imagine, and innovate.

4. FOURTH LEVEL: MOTIVE POWER BASED ON PURE CONCEPTUAL THINKING

Steiner indicates that the fourth level of human life is pure conceptual thinking which provides the "highest level" of motive power, as I noted above. We can act on this level when we are capable of pure, intuitive thinking, independent of any perceptual content from our drives, habits, emotions, and past experience. What motivates us to act is the intuition of a thought or ideal, pure and simple, which we intuit in the moment or in the course of thoughtful reflection, which latter Steiner terms "practical reason," following a philosophical tradition.

Motive power on this level comes from one's present-time understanding of what is right or appropriate to do. The power is in the understanding gained in thinking about a present situation and what to do about it. It is an energy that fills one in the moment when understanding occurs, a "eureka!" moment, an "I know what to do" moment. Compare that with a feeling leading me to act, or a natural drive. In those cases, thinking is not active, the I is not acting out of its own nature as a thinker.

When I was an elementary school teacher, I had an eight-year-old boy in my class who had a lot of energy and could not sit still for long. My verbal responses intended to refocus his attention had very little effect, until one day after some thought about him I had an intuition, an insight of my own. I said to him, "Here, Tommy,[39] take my watch and run around the school building for ten minutes, then come back to your desk." When he returned, he settled right down. To give him this permission came to me as an intuition in present time, in the course of my thinking into his nature and needs. I acted at once, as soon as the intuition formed in my mind. It certainly was not a recommended practice in our school to allow a child to run freely, unsupervised in this manner, and no one had ever done so, as far as I knew. But in this case it worked wonders. I believe it is an example of Steiner's fourth level of motive power.

It's important to note here that this level of motive power refers to intuitive thinking as the motivational factor for action, and is not to be confused with the specific intuition, or motive (or aim

---

39 Tommy was not his real name.

of action), arrived at in the activity of thinking. In my example, my motivation was to give his built-up energy an appropriate outlet; my thinking about his energy motivated me to let him do so. (In fact, in my thinking about him, I was able to "enter into" his energy, to unite myself with it and was able to understand it and its needs.) On the other hand, my motive or specific aim was to have him release that energy by running around the building with my watch, the full reason for which I will explain later in this essay.

I believe this example exemplifies what Steiner means when he states that one's intuitive thinking is a spiritual activity of the "I" that *both* enables one to intuit specific aims *and* motivates the will to act.

Steiner next observes that when one is able to act from this level of motivation, one is no longer doing so on the basis of one's fixed characterological disposition, ingrained behavior patterns, and memories. One has, in effect, moved beyond a fixed characterology into a mobile state of presence made possible by one's own thinking power.[40] My own feelings for the boy were also involved, it is true, and they also played a part in my decision. But those feelings were not fixed or automatic factors determining me to act. Further on in Steiner's text he explains the role feeling can and should play in freeing the will.

———

Up to this point in Chapter 9, I have summarized Steiner's analysis of the possible *motive powers* that can induce an act of will. Once again, they are: 1) natural drives and social tact, 2) feelings, 3) thoughts and images derived from past experiences, and 4) the activity of conceptual intuition.

Reflecting on the first three, I can see that they can and mostly do act as determining factors on my will, which arise in me as bodily impulses, emotional responses, and memory images. I then allow myself to be determined in my action by them. In that sense, I am

———

40 Steiner, ibid., p. 144

actually not free. For the will to be truly free, that is, truly *self-determining*, Steiner is indicating that my "I"—expressing itself in my own energy-producing, motivating power of intuitive thinking—must be the determining factor.

Motives of the Will—Steiner's Three Types

Steiner next proceeds to analyze the possible *motives* for any act of will. He states that any motive we choose will take the form either of a *mental picture* or a *pure concept*. As Steiner observed in Chapters 5 and 7 of Part 1, mental pictures have both a perceptual content and a conceptual meaning. They are memories of things previously observed and understood by means of concepts. On the other hand, pure concepts are ideal meanings that refer to some perceptible content (concepts like justice and equality). In Chapter 4 of Part 1, Steiner observes that "words cannot say what a concept is. Words can only make us notice that we have concepts."[41] With this statement, I believe he implies that pure concepts are themselves pre-verbal intuitions. To think, or intuit, a pure concept is to achieve an understanding not yet put into words: a knowing that has then to express itself by finding the right words. That is my understanding of his use of the terms "concept" and "intuition" at present.

Steiner distinguishes between three *types* of motives that a person can choose to direct his will. To begin with, he refers to all three of these types of motives, using the term "motives of morality."[42] He does not explain why he has chosen this expression. From what follows in the text, he seems to me to be referring to motives of our will which are aimed at some form of the "good," perhaps for me, for others, for the environment or the natural world in general. Hence his use of the term "motives of morality," for by morality we usually mean a sense of and dedication to the good as opposed to the bad or evil. It may well be the case that whenever we will to do anything we are in fact aiming at what for us is some kind of good, although some

41 Steiner, ibid., p. 49
42 ibid., p. 144

kind of evil may unexpectedly result. That is not to say that there are no purposeful evil motives and actions, but I do not think that Steiner is referring to such motives here.

THE FIRST MOTIVE TYPE—PLEASURE

The first type of motive he mentions has to do with *pleasure seeking*, which for most people is certainly thought to be a "good." An example of this motive could be the goal of seeking healthy exercise by means of body surfing at the beach, which I really enjoy doing. Such morally directed pleasure motives as this are held in the mind as mental pictures of the "good" I am aiming to experience. Further, Steiner also describes this kind of motive as "egoistic," that is, as primarily oriented towards my own enjoyment. He indicates that such motives may involve doing good for others, too, but ultimately one's motive is to obtain personal pleasure in doing so.

What separates this first from the other two *types* of motives is the fact that the latter two involve pure concepts rather than being based on mental pictures with a perceptual content (like body surfing or a tasty dish of pasta). Steiner refers to these pure concepts as "moral principles."

THE SECOND MOTIVE TYPE—
PRINCIPLES OF CONSCIENCE

Steiner's second type of motive includes those moral principles that we derive from external authorities, such as parents, teachers of religion, religious texts, the state, and social customs. The Golden Rule would be a prime example. For Steiner, this second kind of motive takes on a specific, more developed form in what we call our moral "conscience." He indicates that in acting from conscience alone, a person can be said to have gained moral *autonomy* from the dictates of others, although from what he goes on to describe as the third type of motive, I think that for him motives of conscience are based on those moral principles which are ingrained in us and arise like memories, or reminders from our upbringing, in dealing with specific situations. They are not motives arrived at through present-time intuition.

THE THIRD MOTIVE TYPE—MORAL INSIGHT

The third type of motive that Steiner describes is not derived from external authority or conscience but from what he calls one's "moral insight." At this level, Steiner writes, "we consider the *needs* of a moral life and allow our actions to be determined by knowledge of them."[43] He mentions two such needs: the "greatest possible welfare of humanity" and the "progress of civilization." Examples of such motives could be: (1) Promoting the "general welfare" by producing inexpensive plastic goods to meet everyday needs (bottles, toys, phones, computers), or (2) providing for progress in the standard of living through mass production of such goods. They aim not just for the good of oneself or a few others but for society in general.

Steiner then proceeds to distinguish three levels of moral insight which, I believe, pertain to a person's level of self-development, as in his analysis of motivational levels above[44].

MORAL INSIGHT—LEVEL ONE

Steiner characterizes persons on the first level of moral insight as those who base their actions on *one standard moral principle alone* and who "strive to do whatever they think will most promote (it)." Steiner alludes to the fact that such singular "insight" into the needs of moral life, could result in many different, unintended, perhaps even conflicting or destructive actions in social, political, and economic life. As he puts it, in choosing to act only on the principle of the greatest possible welfare, a person "will have to accept into the bargain the demise and destruction of many things that also contribute to the welfare of humanity."[45] However, such a person's motive will still be based on, and be justified by, that particular moral principle. An example from recent history would include the development

43 Steiner, ibid,. P. 146
44 Ibid., p. 56ff
45 Ibid., p. 146

and expansion of the hydrocarbon and plastics industries, justified as contributing to the general welfare or the progress of civilization, yet, as it turns out, resulting in destructive climate change and environmental degradation. The actual moral value of such motives and actions is questionable, however much they are meant to embody a general moral principle.

MORAL INSIGHT—LEVEL TWO

Steiner indicates that the first kind of moral insight, based on one fixed principle or standard, is not the highest form of moral insight. He writes that a "higher form of moral insight" occurs when individuals do not identify with a specific moral standard to be applied in all of one's actions, but first reflect on and then choose from among different standards depending on the situation. Thus a person might choose to act in such a way as to promote progress, or the general welfare, or one's own personal welfare. But here, too, the ultimate moral integrity of doing so depends on the concrete situation and its effects, which could turn out to be negative.

However, it is obvious to me that Steiner's concern here is not to emphasize the possible immoral outcome of actions based on one or another moral principle. His focus in this Chapter on the idea of free will is to show to what extent one is able to realize true freedom of action. For him the main issue is to show to what degree one has achieved freedom at these three levels of so-called moral insight.

Regarding the first two levels of moral insight, Steiner implies that such moral principles as social welfare or economic progress are sufficiently general as to be applied to all sorts of situations and endeavors. But they are not derived from an *individual's specific insight* into the right solutions for *particular* social and personal needs and situations. They are general standards with no specificity, and they are often learned from others, or are part of common ethical or democratic values which have been taught and acquired from others. A person may well gain an understanding or insight into the moral quality of such principles, but the point is that these first two "levels" do not necessarily help one in deciding on specific actions. For Steiner, acting on the basis of such general, externally derived or "outer" standards, as he also describes them, could mean that one is in fact not free on these two levels. That would be the case if one has not gained one's motive for a *specific* action through one's *own* insight, but rather from others. Or, it could be that such motives are connected to those motivating factors arising from ones' natural drives, emotions, or past experience, which are not freely self-determining factors of the will in Steiner's view, as mentioned above.

MORAL INSIGHT—LEVEL THREE

For Steiner, the third and highest level of moral insight is not achieved through reference to one's accepted, general moral principles, whether it be one standard alone or through choice among several. Rather, the highest moral insight flows from an individual's "moral intuition," in the moment. As he puts it, what differentiates a moral intuition from the first two kinds of moral insight just described is that a specific moral intuition is not determined by previously conceived general standards and actions based on them. A moral intuition is won through one's own thinking into specific situations and their moral needs. Moral intuition is for Steiner the highest level of motive of the will of which we are capable and is the only motive that enables the will to be truly free.

My motive to have Tommy run around the school with my watch in ten minutes is for me an example, however insignificant, of such a moral intuition. It came to me as a suitable way to allow him to release his energy given the classroom situation, his own nature, and what we were studying at the time. I did not follow accepted ways of maintaining classroom discipline which I had been taught, nor the advice of other teachers, but my own insight into the needs of the moment.

————

In describing the kinds of *motive power* earlier in the Chapter, Steiner indicated that the inner *activity of intuition* is the highest level of motive power, as it provides us with the impulse to act derived from the free, self-sustaining activity of our own thinking. Now, in regard to the second characteristic of any act of will, namely the motive or specific aim of our action, he has indicated that the highest level of motive is that which is gained from the activity of our intuition in meeting specific situations. To this result Steiner now adds the following "reflection":

> We described the stage of characterological disposition that works as pure thinking, or practical reason, as the highest (form of motive power). We have now described conceptual intuition as the highest motive. More exact reflection soon reveals that motive power and motive coincide at this level of morality.[46]

I think Steiner can say that motive power and motive "coincide" at this level of willing because the motive arrived at is itself the intuitive content arising within one's intuitive activity. *What determines me to act is my own thinking activity and my own concept of what specifically I will do.* If I am responding to a situation that I have come upon, I will do so on this level not because that situation itself reminds me of a moral standard that I should follow in responding to that situation, but because I have myself intuited what I take to be the appropriate moral action to take. To achieve this level of willing depends on being able to think intuitively.

Steiner does not say here how this ability is developed. He only says the following:

> People vary in their capacity for intuition. For one person ideas just bubble up, while another achieves them by much labor. The situations in which people live, and which serve as the scene of their activity, are no less varied. How I act will therefore depend

---

46 Steiner, ibid., p. 148

on how my capacity for intuition works in relation
to a particular situation. The sum of ideas active
within us, the real content of our intuitions, consti-
tutes what is individual in each of us, notwithstand-
ing the universality of the world of ideas. To the
extent that the intuitive content turns into action,
it is the ethical content of the individual. Allowing
this intuitive content to live itself out fully is the
highest driving force of morality. At the same time, it
is the *highest motive*..... We can call this standpoint
ethical individualism.[47]

One could conclude from Steiner's analysis of motive power
and motive thus far that the conditions for achieving free will are
1) being able to think intuitively and 2) deriving one's motives for
action from that ability. However, Steiner now adds one more condition for that highest level of willing to occur. We will find two more
conditions beyond this third one, described in Chapter 12. But now,
still in Chapter 9, he goes on to say that an act of free will depends
above all on *one's love for the action.*

What directs me (in my action) is not common
usage, not general custom, not a universal human
principle and not an ethical norm, but *my love for
the deed.* I feel no compulsion, neither the compulsion of nature, which guides me in my drives, nor
the compulsion of ethical commandments. I simply
want to carry out what lies within me.[48]

In other words, it is my love for my intuited action which truly
frees me when acting from the motive power of intuitive thinking and an intuited motive, for then, as Steiner writes, "I feel no

47   Ibid., p. 150
48   Steiner, ibid., p. 151-2

compulsion" in my actions. Clearly, when I love or "simply want" to do something, I do not feel a foreign element compelling me to do so. Rather, my own feeling is my guiding impulse.

This third condition for an action to be freely willed has to do more with motive power than with motive. Love is a kind of motivation rather than a motive itself. A person could say to another, "My aim is to love you" (meaning that is my motive). But, in fact, if the feeling of love is not there, it is a fruitless motive. As a motivating feeling, love goes together with the motivating power of intuition; love could be said to be the "special quality" of intuition that enables me to feel truly free in any action.

I can see why Steiner includes "love for the deed" as a third condition of free willing, given what he wrote earlier in Chapter 6 (Human Individuality), concerning our "dual nature" and our "true individuality." As I mentioned in that Chapter summary, he states that "thinking and feeling correspond to the dual nature of our being." He adds that "our thinking unites us with the world; our feeling leads us back into ourselves and makes us individuals." On the following page he then asserts that "a true individual will be the person who reaches highest, with his or her feelings, into the region of ideals," thus uniting these two aspects of our being human.[49] While he does not say so at that point in the text, this reaching with one's personal feelings towards ideals most likely will involve the feeling of love for them, which turns out to be an essential ingredient for free will later in his text.

It occured to me when Steiner first characterized the highest level of motive power as intuitive thinking, he also had in mind that a part of that level must also include the feeling of love, though he did not mention it at that point in Chapter 9. And, as I reflect on the nature of intuition, it seems to me that it itself must involve, at least in part, a "love experience" that could be termed a "feeling-at-one-with." In

---

49   ibid. p. 101-2

fact, I think it very likely that intuition in any situation is only possible for one who is able to unite with that situation as one does when one loves something.

For instance, when I had the intuition to allow Tommy to leave the room and run around the building, I had at the same time connected more deeply and sympathetically with him (really a form of love for him), a feeling that may have enabled my intuition to "bubble up." However, there was also thinking involved, not just feeling. Intuitions bubble up in and for thinking.

In Part 1 of his book Steiner observed that our thoughts are all interconnected through their meanings. For example, triangles and squares have meanings that show their connection. They both have sides and angles, though different in number. Thinking about them, another geometrical figure comes to mind: a trapezoid. My thinking can generate all the other possible multi-sided figures as well. This is a clue to understanding how intuition is possible.

Intuition is possible just because our thoughts all have connections to other thoughts. Thinking dives into this interconnected "web of thoughts" and discovers, or intuits, other thoughts related to those under consideration. Thinking about Tommy led me to thoughts of how best to deal with his restlessness. My specific intuition came to me from this "web of connected thoughts." It bubbled up in the moment as the intuition to have him run around the school with my watch.

The situation was different when I once met a beggar in the street of a Mexican town on my way home from the market. I had seen how people would give some money to the beggars, and I had done so myself out of compassion. Each time I did, I also thought about and felt my human kinship with the beggar. This new beggar had no legs, powerful shoulders and arms, and a fierce, aggressive expression as he dragged himself along the street, clutching a basket in which he had collected some coins. As I approached him, he sneered at me and turned away. "Was it because I am a gringo," I wondered, "a foreigner whom he immediately disliked?" I had some coins, but he was not about to let me share them with him. And so I passed him by, but I have never forgotten him. Actually, it was hard for me to feel at one with a sneer like that, though I felt compassion for his situation. I had no intuition of my own of what to do for him, and I think now it was because I was not in that moment able to care enough for him to think into his situation. Perhaps he sensed that. To be honest, he kind of scared me.

Fear would be on the second level of motive powers, the level of feeling. It and our other so-called "negative" feelings (like hatred or greed) may well motivate a person to act in some way, but only in a manner that is compelled by the object of fear or longing. Love is also on the second level of motive powers, for it too is a feeling. But love is a positive force of connecting and can enable one to see right into a situation. It provides the energy to do so. Perhaps that is an essential characteristic of intuitive knowing.....needed so as to unite oneself with things and their meanings, in and through thinking.

However, there is a common saying: "Love is blind." That statement assumes that our affection prevents us from seeing the reality of a situation. How could that love be a condition for free will? I assume that Steiner regarded the love to which he refers as being illuminated by the third level of moral insight based on one's intuition. It is what he would term a spiritual love, for intuition is an activity of the "I," our spirit.

———————

At this point Steiner has spelled out three conditions for achieving free will. These involve the development, even transformation, of one's personality and characterological disposition, so that one can live on the fourth level of motivational power and the third level of moral insight. How does one get there? Through developing the capacity of intuitive thinking. How does one do this? It seems to me that love is at least part of the answer, through being a practice of uniting oneself empathetically with people, with nature, and with life situations of all kinds. This means observing all of that with one's complete attention and interest. And, at the same time, being open in one's thinking, being nonjudgmental. By asking questions and being receptive so that answers may come, and intuitions may "bubble up."

Unfortunately, Steiner does not describe how one can develop intuition, except perhaps indirectly by cultivating and strengthening one's thinking. What he does next in Chapter 9 is deal with the objections that others may have to his view of free will and what he terms "ethical individualism," referred to in the quotation above.

OBJECTIONS TO STEINER'S ETHICAL INDIVIDUALISM

1. First, he refers to the view that if people were left to themselves to determine their motives in life, without clear moral standards applicable to all, chaos would result. He mentions the philosopher Immanuel Kant who conceived his "Categorical Imperative" so that immoral deeds could be avoided. Kant considered it to be the "supreme principle of morality":

"Act only according to that maxim whereby you can, at the same time, will that it should become a universal law."[50] I interpret this to mean: "What you decide is moral should only be what everyone would and should decide is moral,," or, - "what you decide to do, would and should be what everyone should decide to do."

Steiner does not entirely disagree with this principle. It is appropriate for those who have not yet achieved the ability for moral intuition. For them a universal standard is needed to keep their motivational powers, including drives, feelings, and mental pictures (imagination) within moral bounds, so that they do no harm.[51] For this reason, Kant believed, people must obey his "Imperative": It is our Moral Duty to do so. To this Steiner replies, "The simple concept of duty excludes freedom, because duty does not recognize individuality but demands instead subjection of individuality to a general norm. Freedom of action is thinkable only from the standpoint of ethical individualism."[52]

---

50   Immanuel Kant, Groundwork of the Metaphysics of Morals, 1785
51   Steiner, ibid., p. 152
52   Ibid., p. 154

Steiner then clarifies what he means by the term "ethical individ-ualism." An *ethical* individual is a person who has developed beyond the average human being who is still swayed by physical drives, nega-tive feelings, exclusively egoistic desires, and intentions harmful to others. He is one who is able to intuit aims of actions which are truly moral and that he, as an individual, feels connected with and *wants* to achieve. Moreover, Steiner thinks that the actions of such a person will not conflict with other ethical individuals because the intuitions they receive from the "Ideal" realm will be in harmony with his own.

> My neighbors want to live out *their* intuitions, I *mine*. If we all really draw from the Idea, and follow no external (physical or spiritual) impulses, then we cannot but meet in the same striving, the same intentions. An ethical misunderstanding, a clash, is impossible among ethically *free human beings*.... To live in love of action, and to let live in understand-ing of the other's will, is the fundamental maxim of free human beings. They know no other "should" than the one with which their willing is intuitively in harmony. Their capacity for ideas tells them how they are to *will* in any given case..... Only because individuals are of one spirit can they live out their lives side by side. A free person lives in trust that the other free person belongs to the same spiritual world and that they will concur with each other in their intentions.[53]

What Steiner wrote about earlier (in Chapter 3), may help in understanding this quote. There he indicated that as thinking beings we participate in the same spiritual activity, and we thereby have access to the same thought world which enables mutual understand-ing. To me this implies that we can be, at least potentially, "of one spirit" while being at the same time separate, individual spirits.

---

53 Steiner, Ibid., p. 155

2. Steiner next anticipates a second objection to his point of view: the belief that the concept of an ethical individual is a "chimera" : No humans exist who have attained this state or who are capable of it. Steiner acknowledges the relative truth of this opinion of human nature, but states that it is not the final truth of the matter. He considers the free spirit as the "purest expression of human nature" of which we are indeed capable, once we have "discovered the concept of the free spirit" as he has outlined it in this Chapter.[54] He states that we humans are *incomplete* beings. Our true concept does not yet conform to what we perceive and conceive of ourselves as natural beings, and it is up to us to "lift ourselves up" to that concept and make it our reality. Some have achieved this. Others can strive to do so for it is the "final stage of human evolution"[55] to which all can aspire.

3. Steiner next refers to a further possible objection to his ideal of the free spirit or ethical individual: such a person may be regarded by many as a "dangerous person," dangerous, that is, to the existing moral laws and legal requirements of society and the state. Steiner responds to such a concern by saying that existing laws and regulations are for the most part the result of intuitions arrived at in the past by individuals who were concerned with safeguarding ideals of social justice and individual rights. Ethical individuals would not disagree with them or seek to change them unless such laws were in fact undermining those ideals. As he puts it:

> "If they believe that they have better intuitions, then they try to substitute their own for the existing ones; if they find that the existing ones are justified, then they act in accordance with them as if they were their own."[56]

There are many examples of this gradual change of the legal systems in countries around the world. And there are many people who now regard aspects of our own political and economic order

54   Ibid., p. 157
55   Ibid., p. 159
56   Ibid., p. 161

as unjust to the majority and are striving to make changes, while defenders of the status quo seek to stop them.

9. Brief Summary

Steiner's "ethical individualism" may be summed up in the following quotation written towards the end of the Chapter:

> Humans remain in an incomplete state if they do not take in hand the transformative substance within themselves, and transform themselves through their own power. Nature makes human beings merely natural creatures; society makes them law-abiding actors; but they can only make themselves into free beings. At a certain stage of their development, nature releases human beings from her chains; society carries this development up to a further point; but human beings must give themselves the final polish.[57]

Clearly, Steiner believes humans have the power to transform themselves: "characterological disposition" is malleable and capable of development. As we have seen, it requires that one recognizes the levels on which we normally live our lives as we respond to our natural drives, our feelings, and our mental images, all of which can motivate our actions. And, instead of allowing these motivators to determine what we do, we need to cultivate intuitive thinking, as the means of gaining moral insight as to the right thing to do, based on our sense of the morally good and our love for the means we intuit to achieve it.

10. Freedom-Philosophy and Monism

In this Chapter, Steiner describes his view of free will in terms of Monism, his epistemological orientation which he presented in Part 1 of his book. He again contrasts his monistic outlook with Naive

---

57   Ibid., p. 159

Realism and Metaphysical Realism, but this time he does so in terms of their conception of human willing. He shows how and why free will is impossible for both viewpoints.

A naive realist is one who believes that his knowledge is based solely on what he can perceive by means of his physical sense organs. Thus, he thinks that what he knows has been given to him only in that manner, and he has played no part in it. Thinking for him has no role except in forming mental pictures of the sense world. In a similar way, he lets his willing be directed by perceivable guides and authority figures, or, if he regards them as being "as weak as he regards himself," he turns to spiritual teachers, past or present, for their instruction instead. Being so dependent on others, he is unfree in his actions.

A metaphysical realist is one who posits a divine authority in a metaphysical world which is not perceivable and from whom he derives his motives and rules of behavior, which he finds in sacred writings or learns from spiritual teachers. Doing so, he considers himself free from his natural drives, personal feelings, and other unsavory influences. Steiner points out that he is nonetheless unfree, as is the naive realist, for he has not determined these motives and rules for and by himself.

If we base our willed actions purely on the dictates of authority figures, including spiritual authorities, or on metaphysical ideas and so-called sacred writings and instructions, we are also unfree. A monist is one who bases his actions on motive powers and motives that are a part of his own nature and are present in and for his own intuitive activity. Only such a person has achieved real freedom in his or her willing. In Steiner's view, every human being has the potential to achieve such a free will, once having understood the conditions for that achievement.

A monist, on the other hand, recognizes that his knowledge is based on perceptions and concepts. His perceptions arise by means of his sense organs; his concepts by means of his own inner activity of thinking. He or she understands that percepts alone do not ensure an understanding of the world. Concepts provide understanding through the fact that they identify and relate percepts into intelligible wholes and systems. The objects and their relationships that we thus come to know make up our world. We have no way of knowing what we do not perceive and conceive ourselves. If we conceive of an object that we have not perceived in some manner, it is nothing more that a "thing-in-itself," empty of content and unverifiable. Like the metaphysical realist, we have philosophized into thin air.

11. *World Purpose and Life Purpose* (*Human Destiny*)

In this next Chapter Steiner pits his Monism against Metaphysical Realism in terms of a specific concept related to human volition, the concept of *purpose*.

Steiner argues that this concept applies *only* to human volition. *The purpose of any act of will is equivalent to its motive or aim, and that is the only case in which the concept of purpose is applicable.* Steiner objects to the fact that this concept is sometimes used in relation to events other than our willing. For example, it is said that there is a purpose of world history or that there is a purpose for certain natural forms, like the horns of a bull. Such statements assume either (1) a conscious being forming those purposes or (2) an ingrained, purposeful intention in the flow of history or in the forming of a bull's horns. The second assumptions are metaphysical notions.

Steiner reasons that any claim for the presence of a purpose must have a perceptible content, otherwise it is not verifiable. We do not perceive a being in the flow of history, intending its course; we only assume its presence, based on the model of our own purposeful activity. Neither can we perceive an ingrained intention or aim in the forming of a bull's horns or in any other formation in nature. We can perceive purpose only in our own willing activity: it is present for us in the form of an intuition and a related mental picture or image of our intuited motive or aim. We form it in our minds prior to, and, perhaps also, while acting. Our achieved aim is the result or effect of our action. Thus it can be said that our aim both precedes and follows our action, as both a purpose and an effect.

Steiner points out that the cause–effect relations that we grasp in any other kind of events, using our thinking, are not equivalent to purposeful relations. My example: We perceive lightning striking a tree and the tree then charring and splitting into pieces. We do not perceive the lightning intending to strike the tree in a purposeful manner. Rather, our thinking explains the event causally by reasoning that the lightning's electrical charge was grounded through the object closest to it, not by intention (or on purpose) but by the necessity of restoring a positive–negative balance in polarity between earth and atmosphere. Thus, we use the concept of electric polarity balance to explain the relation of two events, the lightning strike and the tree's igniting and/or splitting—the first being the perceived cause of the other. Like all cause–effect relationships, it is a *conceived* one linking two perceived events. And we acknowledge that this conception makes clear, or adequately explains, the reality of the occurrence, at least as far as we know now. It is an example for us of a natural law: Where there is an imbalance in polarity of positive and negative electrical charges, a rebalancing must occur. In this example, the "proximate" cause of the tree splitting is the lightning. The "final" cause is the necessity of rebalancing charges.

Our free, purposeful activity is not bound by such natural law. Cause and effect in our willed actions, purpose and result, do not occur by natural necessity but by our own intentions and will power. We do not or should not include our natural drives, like our breathing, eating, and drinking, as examples of purposeful activity for they work in us as necessities of bodily survival. It is our bodily nature that breathes, eats, and drinks and it does so not because we freely propose to do such things. We are only free to modify how and when to do so, even if it results in death. Our purposeful activity is not, in the end, ruled by any necessity of action. We bring something about because we want to: That is our motivation.

12. *Moral Imagination*

Steiner now proceeds to add the two further conditions for achieving free will to which I referred earlier. He terms these conditions Moral Imagination and Moral Technique, and he describes them in the first part of the Chapter. In the second part of the chapter, he relates his overall view of the nature of free will to the theory of evolution, developed by Charles Darwin and Ernst Haeckel, a theory that had become accepted in his day, at least in academic circles, and has become more generally so today.

MORAL IMAGINATION

Steiner indicates that implementing a specific moral intuition (a motive) through an act of will requires that one forms a definite mental picture of the deed in advance. This will make clear the manner in which the intuition is to be realized. In the simple example I gave above, I indicated the way in which I gave my restless student, Tommy, permission to leave the classroom. My intuition was that he needed some way to settle himself, something physical to do outside in fresh air. I then formed a picture in my mind of him running around the building and conveyed this to him in words. That is a simple example of a moral imagination: I imagined it, considering it as a means to do him some good in a way that he would appreciate.

I believe Steiner would consider my intuition and my mental picture to have been freely formulated. The intuition came to me as I pondered Tommy's restlessness that day. It did not compel me to act; I chose to do so. I then imagined a specific way for him to resolve that restlessness. Had I instead come up with a plan I had learned in my training, I would not have been acting freely in Steiner's view. Such a plan would have been an example of moral imagination in relation to classroom discipline, but it would not have been my own, arrived at in that specific situation unless, of course, such a plan appeared to me, intuitively, as appropriate in Tommy's case. I had on previous occasions considered methods I had learned from others and tried them out. They were sometimes successful, and I came to see the reason for them. In Tommy's case, I knew they would not succeed in helping him to control himself, and so I acted on my own intuitive sense of his needs and character.

MORAL TECHNIQUE

Tommy was an athletic child, and he was basically respectful of his teachers. My technique was to give him a physical and a mental challenge that he would recognize and want to meet as best he could. He was eight years old and had just learned how to tell time, a topic we had been studying just then. So I gave him my watch and ten minutes to run as many times as he could around the main school building, which happened to be in a country setting surrounded by grassy play areas and woods. His eyes lit up; he could not quite believe he was being allowed to do such a thing. The other children were surprised and wondered if he could do the deed and keep track of the time. They kept their eyes on the classroom clock, and several burst out clapping when he returned, right on time. Not much work got done in those 10 minutes, but it didn't matter. Tommy had run an admirable number of laps around the school. With a big smile, he settled right down and so did the others.

Does this simple example of moral technique measure up to Steiner's way of describing it? He does so as follows: Moral technique involves "the transformation of our world of percepts" in regard to specific situations, to give them "a new form or new direction" in our imagination. Thus it requires an understanding of that world (or field) of perceptions and "the capacity to transform it....without interrupting its coherence in natural law."[58] This sounds like a tall order, and it is just that when the transformation involves something complex, like a remodeling of social, political, and economic forms. In my example, I gave Tommy a new direction in which to apply his pent-up energy, and it enabled him to focus and then to settle down and concentrate in the classroom. I suppose that the natural law, whose "coherence was not interrupted," refers to the cause–effect

58   Steiner, ibid., p. 183

relations involved with Tommy's joy in running as many laps as he could in the time allowed, on the one hand, and his subsequent ability to settle in and focus on our lesson that day, on the other hand.

However, In the case of major personal decisions or social transformations, much more will be involved!

Much later in his life, in 1919, Steiner undertook to describe a new social order for postwar Europe, at the time when the Allies were reshaping national boundaries, punishing the defeated countries and attempting to free subject peoples by creating new nations. His idea has since been called the Threefold Social Order. Steiner was sure it would be a better solution than was being proposed to the problems that had created World War 1 in the first place. It was his intuition and moral imagination at work on a grand scale. He intuited that the social order should be based on three ideals: freedom, equality, and brotherhood. (Had he lived at the present time, I think he would have labelled the third ideal more inclusively as a brother/ sisterhood.) Steiner grasped that freedom should pertain to all cultural endeavors, equality should pertain to the rights of, and legal relations between, individuals, and that brotherhood belongs as a guiding ideal for the means of economic production and the sharing of natural resources. He formed mental pictures of how these ideals could be realized in those spheres of life: the cultural, the political, and the economic. He left the determination of the technique for refashioning those three spheres of life to social and political leaders, though he made several suggestions. However, the victors of World War I were not interested, and nothing was done on such a grand scale to improve human relationships and activities. Since then, there have been successful attempts to implement his principles on a smaller scale within a few countries, in Europe and the Philippines.

EVOLUTIONARY THEORY AND ETHICS

Steiner's second point in Chapter 12 is to describe the relationship of his Ethical Individualism (set forth in Chapter 9) to the theory of evolution developed by Charles Darwin and Ernst Haeckel. He means to show that his ideal of an "ethical Individual" is in harmony with their view of the evolution of living organisms. I think his reasoning can be summarized as follows.

Steiner observes that new moral concepts and imaginations do not develop directly from previous ones. For if previous moral principles developed into later ones, this would mean, for example, that the moral principle of the Categorical Imperative espoused by Kant developed naturally into Steiner's Ethical Individualism. Rather, successive moral principles or concepts arise not from previously established concepts, i.e., *norms*, but from the thinkers who intuit them. A science of ethics cannot predict the ethical concepts that may arise in the future, on the basis of previous ones. What will come in the future will depend on future generations of thinkers giving voice to their own intuitions.

Steiner compares this reasoning to the manner in which Darwin and Haeckel viewed the development of species from less complex to more complex forms. Steiner refers, by way of example, to the relationship between proto-amniotes and reptiles. He states that Darwin and Haeckel did not maintain that their *concept* of the nature of reptiles developed from the *concept* of proto-amniotes. Darwin's and Haeckel's understanding of evolution was conceived of and understood based on the hypothetically perceivable development of real organisms in the past, including the human being. This understanding is in accord with Steiner's epistemological method, basing concepts on our perceptual experience. Steiner now adds that the relation between his own perceived ability of moral intuition and the perceivable moral behavior of his time, based on external authority or a moral principle like the Categorical Imperative, provides a further example of evolution. He conceives it to be a further step in the evolution of humanity which can be brought about by the self-development of individuals.

Darwin and Haeckel viewed humanity as a more developed stage of animal life and the last stage of natural development, at least so far. For Steiner, this further development of the animal nature into the human involves all the human capacities, including intellectual and moral intuition. Thus, Steiner could say that an intuitive human being stands "at the pinnacle" of human evolutionary development so far, both in theory and in fact.

> Thus, ethical individualism does not contradict a theory of evolution when it is properly understood, but follows directly from it. Haeckel's genealogical tree, running from protozoa to human beings as organic beings, ought to be traceable—without interrupting natural law or breaking the uniformity of evolution—right up to the individual as an ethical being in a specific sense.[59]

Steiner goes on to describe this "specific sense." He objects to the interpretation of evolutionary development based on Metaphysical Realism as he has previously described it. The driving force of evolution should not be conceived to exist outside of or beyond the perceivable world, for such a force amounts to no more than an unobservable belief. The real driving force of evolution can be observable in successive, gradually developing organic forms of life, and it can be further observed in human development as well—when specific humans develop in themselves the capacity of intuitive thinking. This capacity is a result of that very force within them, actualizing itself. It is the capacity enabling the human will to act freely, on the basis of intuited aims arrived at through one's own self-sustaining force of thinking.

Steiner ends Chapter 12 by referencing the definition of free will of Robert Hamerling, which he mentioned in Chapter 1. For Hamerling, freedom of action depends on *being able to do what one wills*. Since that Chapter, Steiner has gradually unfolded what it means "to do what one wills" and to do it *freely*. And now at the end of Chapter 12, he describes that *truly free doing* in the activity of moral imagination:

---

59   Steiner, ibid., p. 187

To be free means: to be able—on my own, through moral imagination—to determine the mental pictures (motives) underlying an action. Freedom is impossible if something outside myself (whether a mechanical process or a merely inferred, other-worldly God) determines my moral mental pictures. Therefore, I am free only when I produce these mental pictures myself, not merely when I can carry out motives that another has placed within me. Free beings are those who can will what they themselves hold to be right.[60]

But as I have described in summarizing this and previous Chapters, there is more than just moral imagination involved in free willing. Let me summarize again what I have learned so far of Steiner's conditions for achieving free will. *Moral imagination* is the ability to form specific images of actions, which will enable us to realize our *moral intuitions* of what is *right* for us to do. *Moral technique* is the further ability to transform those images into reality. Our *love for the deed* is the motivational force for acting on our intuitions and specific images of what we intend to achieve. Often we may have to rely on others to help us with moral technique. But the original intuition, the subsequent imagination and our personal love must be our own, produced by our *own free, spiritual activity in thinking* and *imagining* (mental picturing), as well as through our own, quite individual, life of *feeling*.

13. The Value of Life (*Pessimism and Optimism*)

Steiner's aim in writing this next Chapter was to characterize two popular conceptions of the value of life prevailing in his day and to present his own. The first he finds in the philosophical outlook of *Shaftesbury and Leibniz* and the second in the views of *Schopenhauer and von Hartmann* of whom mention has already been made in Part 1

---

60   Steiner, ibid., p. 191

of the book. After he has described the philosophical views of these thinkers, he contrasts them with his own view of the value of life. (Readers may find these conceptions dated and not particularly relevant to our own time. They may think that Steiner's detailed analysis of von Hartmann's reasoning in this Chapter to be more appropriate for an addendum to his book, for it does not seem to relate directly to his theme of free will. Nevertheless, I have attempted to summarize that analysis for the sake of completeness and because, in the end, the reader discovers that life's value equals, for Steiner, the value to us of those goals that we each choose freely to achieve in life.)

These philosophers all assume the existence of God as the creator of the world. The former two, Leibniz and Shaftesbury, believe that God has created the "best of all possible worlds" and humans have the good fortune to enjoy His blessings as long as they perform His will to do good by obeying His commandments. That should be our purpose in life and gives it value. Of the latter two, Schopenhauer believes that God's nature consists of a striving for the satisfaction of desires, which He has also introduced into human nature. Von Hartmann believes that God's nature includes an unbearable degree of pain and suffering that He can never escape, except partially, through sharing that pain with humanity and leaving it to us to help relieve His suffering by suffering along with Him. That should be our human purpose and expresses the value of our life. Obviously, the outlook on human life of the former two is optimistic while that of the latter two is pessimistic.

Steiner then focuses on von Hartmann. Again, the latter's view of human life is that our pain and suffering, predominant in our experience, is unavoidable and necessary in order to relieve God to some extent of His much greater pain. It is our moral responsibility to God to bear this pain nobly, and to accept the inevitability of a life of suffering. The purpose and value of life consists in this.

Von Hartmann's conception of God's nature and purpose is clearly metaphysical, without perceptual verification. It is not Steiner's purpose now to refute it on that basis. Rather, he argues with von Hartmann's assumptions concerning the predominance of pain in human life. He makes several observations and related points that I will summarize. He focuses on von Hartmann's view that all human striving produces pain and that life's pleasures are illusory. I imagine that Steiner decided to do so because von Hartmann's thinking had a considerable influence in Steiner's day, and it needed to be challenged.

Steiner agrees that pain may be involved in human striving towards goals, but he also points to the fact that our striving can also be energizing and can bring pleasure, rather than pain, in the doing, even "independent of attaining our goal." If our striving is fulfilled, then our joy is further enhanced. If not fulfilled, we will still have the recollection of the pleasure we enjoyed in the striving. Further, Steiner points to the additional fact that we also enjoy aspects of life that do not involve our striving, that come unexpectedly. And he disagrees that our pleasures in life are illusory. We actually *experience* pleasure of which only we can be the judge. Then he asks if it is really true, as von Hartmann claims, that pain and suffering predominant in our experience.

Steiner uses the metaphor of a business ledger of gains and losses to seek whether in life we have a surplus of pain on one side of the ledger of life or a surplus of enjoyment on the other side. He asks, what is the "right method for reckoning the balance of these credits and debits?"[61] He goes on to indicate that von Hartmann thinks a rational analysis of the issue is better than one based on feelings, for feelings are merely subjective. That analysis leads Hartmann to conclude that people deceive themselves when they think that their efforts and accomplishments bring them pleasure. For example, a rational person will eventually realize that any ambition he feels for achievement in life will color his experience and mistakenly lead him to emphasize the pleasure and minimize the pain he feels from his efforts. Once he has freed himself from such ambition, he will realize that his pleasure has been eclipsed by pain. Moreover, since

---

61   Steiner, ibid., p. 201

one's sense of achievement is largely due to recognition by others, he will realize that any pleasure gained from such recognition is in fact worthless, which only exacerbates the pain felt from his efforts.

Rudolf Steiner disagrees with this "rational" analysis, because in his view it is not true to life; that is, it does not value the way people actually feel about their efforts and accomplishments, even when their pleasure depends on the response of others. One cannot deny that one has felt pleasure prior to such analysis. As Steiner puts it, "If it is merely a question of weighing the relative quantities of pleasure and pain, then such a "rational" judgment of the illusory character of certain feelings of pleasure should be left completely out of the picture." Thus he questions whether "reason is equipped to reckon the balance."

Steiner reminds the reader that all cognition depends as much on percepts as it does on reason and concepts. The feelings of pleasure and pain are themselves percepts, and their value in the reckoning cannot therefore be discounted. Otherwise, such "estimating a pleasure at a lower rate because it attaches to a worthless object (e.g., to recognition from others) is like a merchant who enters in his ledger the considerable profits of a toy factory at a quarter of their worth, on the grounds that the factory produces mere playthings for children."[62] A clever analogy!

Anyone who agrees with von Hartmann's view that pain outweighs pleasure, might well conclude that a rational solution to this dilemma would be to commit suicide. Yet, Steiner observes, few people resort to this. Von Hartmann evidently did not do so because of his metaphysical conviction that the suffering of God is alleviated by our own suffering and pain. Human endurance of a painful life is for him a moral obligation to God. However, Steiner points out that for others, it may well be that the value of life is based on their calculation of a surplus balance of pleasure over pain. Which calculation is correct? Steiner then proceeds to describe his own method of estimating the value of life in relation to *the various drives in which our life "expresses" itself*, and the pleasure which they can provide us.

---

62   Steiner, ibid., p. 205

(Recall here Steiner's analysis of the four levels of our characterological disposition in Chapter 9, the first being the level of our drives.)

He then describes ways in which we should value the pleasure gained from our drives or instincts. For example, the value of the pleasure derived from a specific drive, like hunger, can be calculated relative to its own present time satisfaction, or to its satisfaction over time. Specifically, he writes:

> Our shares in life's pleasure in the form of instincts fall in value when we cannot hope to cash them in for the full amount. If I have enough to eat for three days and then must go hungry for the next three, the pleasure of those three days of eating is not diminished. But I must think of it as distributed over the six days, so that its value in terms of my food drive is reduced to one half. It is the same with the amount of pleasure in relation to the *degree* of my need. If I have enough hunger for two pieces of buttered bread but I only get one, then the pleasure derived from it has only half of the value that it would have if I had been satisfied by that one piece alone. This is how the value of pleasure in life is determined. It is measured against life's needs. *Our desires are the yardstick; pleasure is what we measure....* A quantity of pleasure has full value for us when its duration and degree exactly correspond with our desire. When it is smaller than our desire, the value of a given quantity of pleasure is diminished; when the pleasure is greater, we have an undesired surplus, which is felt as pleasure only for as long as we can heighten our desire during the enjoyment itself. If we are in no position to keep the growth of our desire in step with the increase of pleasure, then pleasure turns into displeasure....

> This is one proof that pleasure has value for us only
> as long as we can measure it against our desire. [63]

Steiner recognizes that the fulfillment of many of our desires involves experiencing pain as well as pleasure. The question then is, how do we determine if our anticipated pleasure is worth it, even if the pain can be excessive? Again, we measure the pain against the *degree* of our desire. He gives the painful experience of childbirth as an example. The mother's desire to have a child and the anticipated joy in having one outweighs the pain involved. As he puts it, "The question is never whether pleasure or pain is present in surplus but whether the *will* for the pleasure and its object is great enough to overcome the pain."[64]

Steiner thinks that pessimists like von Hartmann believe that once we humans realize the impossibility of a life of pleasure and happiness, we will follow their lead and dedicate our lives selflessly to the moral goal of alleviating God's suffering. Steiner's view is that "the human will, by its very nature, is not influenced by this knowledge." Humans will continue to seek pleasurable objects and outcomes, based on their natural *and spiritual* drives, even if the pain of doing so is hard to bear. He regards the pessimistic point of view as based on an abstraction of the pleasure–pain dynamic from actual reality.

> The claim that humans strive merely for happiness
> is the invention of a philosophy gone astray. We
> strive for satisfaction of what our essential nature
> desires, and we have in view the concrete objects
> of this striving and not some abstract "happiness."
> Fulfillment of such striving is a pleasure. When
> pessimistic ethics demands that you strive, not for
> pleasure, but for what you have recognized as your
> life's task, it is pointing to what humans by their

63   Steier, ibid., p. 212
64   Steiner, ibid., p. 215

nature *want*. Humans do not need to be turned
upside down by philosophy; they do not need to
throw away their nature to be ethical. Morality lies
in striving for a goal recognized as just; and it is
human nature to pursue the goal as long as the pain
involved does not cripple the desire for it. This is
the nature of all real willing.[65]

Human nature for Steiner includes "natural and spiritual desires."
Our natural desires are focused on physical needs, like food, shelter,
warmth, and physical pleasure. Our spiritual desires are related to
the realization of our ideals, like beauty, truth, and goodness, in our
lives and deeds. In his view, ethical conduct may well involve the
control or denial of some of our bodily impulses aimed at physical
pleasure, but that is not necessary as long as they are not harmful.
He is concerned with the "full development of human nature." We
can develop our spiritual capacity for intuition and imagination and
our ability to control those natural impulses that are harmful to self
and others. And we can thereby realize our spiritual values freely,
without being told what to do or by obeying duties and commandments imposed on us from without. Thus he writes in his concluding
paragraph to the Chapter:

> The view developed here returns us to ourselves.
> It recognizes as the true value of life only what we
> individually regard as such according to the mea-
> sure of what we want. It knows of no value in life
> that is not recognized by the individual, just as it
> knows of no life goal that does not spring from the
> individual. It sees our own master and our own
> assessor in the essential individuality of each of us,
> seen into from all sides.[66]

---

65   Ibid., p. 219
66   Steiner, ibid., p. 223

He refers here to our "essential individuality, seen into from all sides." I take him to mean by "all sides" our threefold nature: our thinking, feeling, and willing capacities.

14. Individuality and Genus

In this next Chapter Steiner takes up a theme that at first may seem to be more related to human cognition than to human volition. One might think, as I did at first, that it could well have been a Chapter in Part 1 of the book. However, it is entirely appropriate here, for it involves the specific nature and requirements of cognition in coming to understand a person's quite individual motives and motivation in life.

We all bear characteristics determined by the nature of the groups of which we are a part. For instance, we seek to explain aspects of individual physiognomy and even of the activities in which people engage by referring to the group or "whole" to which they belong. Such groups include our race, tribe, people, family, profession, and male or female gender. I would add that our so-called natural drives, which include breathing, hunger, thirst, and our sexual instincts, are also of a generic nature. Steiner then states that all human beings also develop "qualities and functions of our own, whose only source can be found within ourselves. What is generic about us serves only as a medium through which we can express our own distinct being."[67]

He next refers to the fact that people do not always seek to understand and know the "distinct being" of other people and even of themselves. In characterizing women, for example, men of Steiner's time often failed to observe their individual natures, and thought of them all as basically the same in nature, with the same role in life, to bear and raise children and "keep house." Men conflated women's individuality with their generic, sexual characteristics as child bearers and thought it appropriate for them to live an exclusively domestic life. Down through history there are women who have also held this view of themselves, while others have struggled against it. This

---

67   Steiner, ibid., p. 226

view was undoubtedly true of Steiner's time (late 19th and early 20th centuries), as it was before then, but is less the case today in much of the industrialized world. Steiner urged men of his own time to recognize that women "must be allowed to decide for themselves what is appropriate to their nature." He was ahead of his time in this respect, an important supportive voice in the just-developing women's movement at the end of the 19th century.

Steiner next refers to the difference between the kind of cognition that seeks a generic understanding of inorganic and organic life processes, on the one hand, and the kind that is necessary to understand a human being's particular individuality. He reminds us of Part 1 of his book, where he explained that "cognition consists of linking a concept with a percept through thinking." In the natural sciences, the concepts that we employ to identify and relate our perceptions of the world and its phenomena are mostly generic. I see something in the darkness of night. I cognize it as an animal, then, on closer inspection, I think it to be a skunk. Animal and skunk are generic concepts; they enable us to "type" the object.

Here is another example: Say I see another person who is extremely upset. I think: He is being hysterical. On reflection, I conclude that because he has behaved like this before, he has a tendency towards hysteria. Those, too, are generic concepts and judgments that I think to be appropriate to explain what I observe. Steiner maintains that such concepts do not go far enough to grasp the individual human beings who, in their volitional life, do what they want to do on the basis of their intuition. To achieve this kind of cognition of the actions of free human beings, one should not depend on concepts about them that one has conceived oneself. Rather, to fully understand another person and his or her actions, I must be able "to bring over into my own spirit in a pure form....those concepts by which the individuality determines itself" in its thoughts, motives, and actions.[68]

For Steiner, as we have seen, a free individual acts from his or her own intuition and imagination. In doing so, the individual is

68 Steiner, ibid., p. 229

not following examples, norms, rules or commandments given from outside. Nor is he or she following impulses having to do with family background or racial characteristics. She or he follows his or her own intuition and understanding, then forms images for actions and carries them out. To understand such a person, we need to be able to intuit, imagine, and act specifically as he or she has. Thus Steiner writes,

> People who immediately mix their own concepts into any judgment of others can never attain an understanding of an individuality. Just as a free individuality frees itself from the characteristics of the genus, cognition must free itself from the approach appropriate to understanding what is generic.[69]

If I judge that someone is behaving hysterically, or has a tendency to do so, I am thinking generically. That may be appropriate when trying to understand a person who is not yet free in Steiner's sense. Then it will be necessary to assess the level of thinking, motive, and motivation of such a person. If he or she is judged incapable of intuition and imagination at a particular time, but is being driven by strong feelings of fear, uncertainty, or betrayal as in the case of an hysteric, then one's generic concept in cognizing the situation is appropriate and may enable one to deal appropriately with the situation.

Further, if I judge someone's actions based solely on some notion of their racial or sexual characteristics (black, white, male, female), then I am also thinking generically and ignoring their inner life of spiritual and personal self-awareness and striving. Steiner is pointing here of the need to look deeper before making any judgments about others. He is clearly not a racist or homophobe in his outlook and respect for the unique individuality of each person, although he has recently been characterized as racist based on certain of his statements concerning the races at the time he lived. I think one always has to bear in mind that he did not think a generic

69 ibid.

analysis of human identity and behavior was the last and final word he would have spoken.

I think the essential point Rudolf Steiner is making in this Chapter is that individuals who are able to achieve all the conditions for free action in life have *de facto* lifted themselves out of their generic characteristics, at least as far as their specific, free acts of volition are concerned. What they do is what they as individuals conceive and want to do, not because of their race, sex, habits, or other generic characteristics. We may continue to view them as members of a certain race, culture and social, or intellectual group, but we should not think that those generic concepts explain their essential being and their willing.

Final Questions

The Consequences of Monism

I have now reached the last Chapter of *Intuitive Thinking as a Spiritual Path: A Philosophy of Freedom*. Steiner did not give it a Chapter number, perhaps because it does not introduce a new topic or theme but rather serves as a summary of what has gone before. There are three key points that Steiner makes in this summary. First, he presents again his Monism as a philosophical position. Second, he explains once more how his monistic view of experience enables us to grasp the full reality of the world that we perceive. Third, he summarizes how Monism applies to human volition and the liberation of the will. To these three explanatory reviews, he adds a fourth indication in the Addendum to the 1918 edition of the book, which has to do with the possibility of spiritual experience beyond the boundary of what we can know with our physical senses. I will summarize each of them in what follows.

1. What is Monism? It is the philosophy that claims that we can obtain an objective knowledge of the world by means of "thinking observation." It differs from Dualist philosophies whose proponents claim that our perceptions and concepts are subjective in nature, produced by our sense organs and the brain. Human subjectivity and the world of objects (beings) are *assumed* to be fundamentally separate and distinct realities. Neither through sense perception nor

through concepts can we gain certain knowledge of the reality of "things-in-themselves." Dualists believe that the physical and biological sciences can only attempt to formulate and test hypothetical explanations of that reality.

Contrary to Dualism, Steiner claims that humans are "not in fact cut off from the world. The individual is a part of the world and has a real connection with the whole cosmos, which is broken only for our perception."[70] In the process of perception, our physical senses perceive the world as separated (or "broken") into distinct things and beings, separate from one another and from our perception of ourselves. From this fact, Dualists mistakenly conclude that this apparent separation of things from one another is *absolute and therefore unbridgeable.*

2. How can Monism assure us that we are not in fact cut off from the world that we perceive, that we are instead part of a unitary web of life forms and lifeless things? Of what does that unitary web consist? According to Steiner, it consists of the unified world of concepts that we access through thinking and in terms of which we grasp the reality of what we perceive through our senses. The essential nature of thinking is that it is neither "subjective" nor "objective." Those are conceptual terms by means of which we differentiate our perceptual experience into *conceived* "subjects" and "objects." By means of other concepts, we identify and explain the interrelationships among the subjects and objects of our experience.

Walking through a forest, I, *as a thinker,* "float" above the scene, as it were, taking note of and identifying all that I perceive, and, if I am really interested, I also take note of the complex web of relationships, comings, goings, and doings of all that I perceive. For example, I think: there would be no such healthy trees here without light, air, earth, and water, without "mother and daughter" trees, without mycelium conduits between them, without healthy soil and minerals, without pollinators, nesters, and diggers, as well as foresters to manage light, nourishment, and growth. My thinking grasps the unity, meaning the "interbeing," of all this diversity. I am not cut off

70 Steiner, ibid., p. 231-2

from it; rather, I, too, partake in it by means of my thinking and perceiving, and I come to know this not through perceiving alone but
through understanding by means of thinking.

Thus Steiner's Monism is, as he puts it, a One World Philosophy,
of which we are a part. This unified world at first appears to us as a
disunity, in the form of our percepts alone, including the percepts
of ourselves, with each percept separate from the others, because of
our various sense organs and our perceived spatial positions. That is
our "apparent world." Its contents are missing identity, definition,
meaning, and connection. It's a confusing world. The "real world" is
found when, through thinking, we discover the meanings and interrelationships and thereby come to know all that is at first concealed
from us in sense perception alone.

Recall that in Chapter 4, Steiner observes that "human consciousness is the stage where concept and observation (perception)
meet and are connected to one another."[71] He then adds that human
consciousness is "a thinking consciousness," by means of which we
make sense of our perceptions. Steiner points to the fact that the
whole process of sense perception and concept intuition goes on
within consciousness, or on the "stage" of consciousness, (a process he later terms the "universal world process" as I mentioned in
my summary of Chapter 6 above). That is, our own subjectivity and
the objects that we perceive and conceive to be separate in physical
space are nonetheless contained *within* the "space" of our thinking
consciousness, along with physical space itself. To put it differently,
when I perceive an object that I identify as an oak tree, I am out
there with the tree, I am at one with it, thinking into it, while standing, at the same time, over here as its observer.

Of course, there are countless things and events *outside* my
individual consciousness at any particular time. But the fact is, all
such things must have been part of *someone's* consciousness at *some*
time. To speak of a "thing-in-itself" that is completely outside of
everyone's consciousness, at *all* times, is, as Steiner says, the result

---

71 Steiner, ibid., p. 52

of philosophizing into thin air. In knowing the world, all that we humans have to go on are our perceptions and our conceptions, all of which provide the content of our thinking consciousness. That is the essence of Steiner's Monism: That for us there is only one reality, in and for human consciousness, expressed through percepts and concepts.

3. How does Steiner's Monist worldview apply to the realization of free will? In a free act of will a concept—that is, a moral intuition, is united with a perceptual image (for a proposed action) in our imagination and then actualized as a perceivable event using some chosen technique. It is an opposite process to the uniting of percept and concept in cognition. In the latter case, percepts appear first in consciousness and are then "grasped" and understood by means of their concepts. Steiner calls that process "intellectual intuition." In the case of the will at its highest level of operation, a motive or aim in the form of a moral concept, a "moral intuition," arises first in consciousness to be then united with the percept of the actual action through which the motive is imagined and realized. It follows that for Monism the will is free at that level, because its motive is freely intuited in the self-sustaining activity of intuitive thinking and freely acted upon in love for the deed. At that level, a person has "risen above" and has perhaps also transformed physical, biological, and fixed characterological or cultural factors that otherwise affect and determine our willing, thus rendering it unfree.

4. In his addendum to this last Chapter of the book, Steiner comments on the possibility of extending the sphere of perception to include percepts that open for us access into experience of the non-physical, or spiritual, world. He observes that anyone who has inwardly perceived her or his own activity in thinking will also have recognized that the energy involved is itself non-physical. That is, it is not dependent on physical forces from the bodily organism, but rather on the spiritual force of the individual exerting itself in thinking. He points out for all who have had this experience that it is "a spiritual percept grasped with no sensory organ."

It is a percept in which the perceiver himself or herself is active; and it is an activity of one's self that is simultaneously perceived. In intuitive thinking, human beings are also transferred into a spiritual world as perceivers.[72]

Steiner's Monism thus applies both to sensory and to super-sensory experiences. Our thinking plays the same role in each sphere, as the power to comprehend both kinds of perception, sensory and super-sensory. In this addendum at the end of the *Philosophy of Freedom*, Steiner indicates that our knowledge can be extended to include perceptions in the realm of spiritual beings and processes, beginning with the perception of our own intuitive thinking. In this way he opens the way to a knowledge of spiritual realities that he spent the rest of his life sharing with his contemporaries and which is available to us today in his writings.

───────

72 Steiner, ibid., p. 242

Conclusion

In writing this essay, I have endeavored to follow Rudolf Steiner's process of describing and defending his view of free will. In doing so, I have been able to experience my own freedom in thinking and doing. This is proof for me that the view of the determinists—that free will is an illusion—is itself a misconception based on an incomplete experience of our activity in thinking and in acting upon the intuited goals we set for our will.

In my introduction to this essay, I suggested that Steiner stands within the "libertarian" tradition of modern philosophical reflection, together with such contemporary philosophers as Robert Kane and Alfred Mele. They also teach that achieving free will depends on a certain inner development and transformation of character. They agree that our character and thinking are not fixed things, determined and driven by a long and complex chain of causes and effects that are beyond our ken, as determinist Sam Harris maintains. We are able to lift ourselves out of that deterministic, causal chain when we achieve the level of personal motivation and moral insight that Steiner indicates.

Steiner describes for us what it takes to be truly free and leaves it to the reader to follow his train of thought, grasp his conditions, and practice them. It is a question of character development that we can achieve by acknowledging the levels on which we lead our lives and by seeking to cultivate the fourth level, which he terms conceptual thinking. Steiner's description of these levels in Chapter 9 can help us to identify and work with them.

Gradually we become able to base our aims and motivation for action on each level of our lives on moral intuition rather than simply on instinctive drives, emotion, habit, custom, and given standards. Though we may not be able to free our will entirely on the instinctive or impulsive levels of our perceiving, feeling, and habitual behavior, we can nonetheless seek motives in response to those levels by means of intuitive thinking, a process that can also modify our aims and motivation on those levels.

Steiner indicates that it is up to us to make such changes by strengthening our thinking powers. Cultivating emotional openness, positivity, appreciation, and love for the world as well as seeking to realize *ideals* in our relationships and activities can also transform our instincts, feelings, and habits. It is for us to cultivate these nascent capacities that are present in all of us to some extent. In this way, we can continue our evolutionary development until we can fully embody the concept of the free spirit as Steiner describes it. We do need to exert ourselves to achieve that freedom, and in thinking we do so freely because our thinking power is already free: only *we* do it, that is, our spiritual "I" power does it and not some mechanism in our physical brain. Steiner stresses that our "I" is our spiritual center, and he urges us to experience this fact. We will then awaken to our own self-engendered and self-sustaining spiritual activity, which is the very basis for achieving a free, moral characterology as Steiner describes it in Part II of his book.

We do strengthen those powers when we are active in cognizing the world as it presents itself to our senses. We also do so when we seek moral (ideal) aims for our will through thoughtful reflection and intuition. As Aristotle wrote centuries ago, "the things we have to learn before we can do them, we learn by doing them."[73] Thinking one's way through Rudolf Steiner's book and applying his indications in our daily lives can be such a doing—through which we can strengthen our intuitive powers and free our will.

---

73 Aristotle, Nicomachean Ethics.

Made in the USA
Middletown, DE
06 May 2023

29764806R00060